nF419563

EASY ASTROLOGY

LEARN IN SIMPLE STEPS

Dr. Mohan Kumar V.V

ISBN
Paperback 979-8-89906-589-7
Hardcase 979-8-89906-954-3

About the Author

Dr. Mohan Kumar V.V an accomplished astrologer and educator, holds a B.Tech in Electrical and Electronics Engineering (EEE), an MBA in Human Resources (HR), an MA, and a PhD in Astrology. With a unique combination of technical expertise and deep astrological knowledge, Dr. Mohan Kumar has successfully guided thousands of individuals through personalized astrological consultations.

Alongside a thriving career as an Electrical Engineer, Dr.Mohan Kumar V.V has dedicated years to practicing and sharing astrological insights. Recognized for their contributions to astrology, they were honoured with the prestigious title "Jyothisha Siromani." Dr. Mohan Kumar V.V has also actively participated in numerous astrological seminars, including notable events across various cities in India and an international Astrological seminar in Malaysia.

Through the popular YouTube channel "VMK Astro-Numerology," with over 300,000 subscribers, Dr. Mohan Kumar V.V educates a broad audience by simplifying complex astrological and numerological concepts and offering practical remedies. Their mission is to make Vedic astrology accessible and understandable to everyone, empowering people to use this ancient science for a better and more fulfilling life.

In *"Easy Astrology: Learn in Simple Steps,"* Dr. Mohan Kumar distills years of experience and knowledge into an easy-to-understand guide, helping beginners navigate the intricate world of Vedic astrology.

Foreword

Astrology has been a guiding force for centuries, offering insights into human nature, relationships, and life's journey. Among the many rich traditions of astrology, Vedic Astrology stands out for its deep connection to ancient wisdom, cosmic rhythms, and spiritual understanding. Yet, for many, navigating this vast ocean of knowledge can feel overwhelming.

"Easy Astrology: Learn in Simple Steps" breaks down these complexities and presents the subject in a way that is accessible, practical, and easy to grasp. Whether you are a curious beginner or someone seeking to deepen your knowledge, this book provides a clear roadmap to understanding the intricate world of planetary movements, zodiac signs, and their influence on our lives.

What makes this book special is its step-by-step approach, designed to demystify Vedic Astrology and empower readers with the confidence to interpret astrological charts, identify key life patterns, and make more informed decisions. The author blends ancient principles with modern insights, ensuring that even complex concepts are made simple and relatable.

As you turn the pages, you will embark on a journey of self-discovery and cosmic exploration. You will learn not only the technical aspects of astrology but also how to apply this wisdom to everyday situations, enriching your life with a deeper sense of awareness and purpose.

I am confident that this book will serve as a valuable companion for anyone eager to explore the secrets of the stars. May your journey through the realms of Vedic Astrology open new doors of understanding and lead you to a path of growth, harmony, and fulfilment.

Thank you for choosing to begin this journey with me

Dr. Mohan Kumar V.V

Astrology has fascinated humankind for ages, offering a glimpse into the mysteries of life and the universe. Among its many branches, Vedic Astrology—deeply rooted in ancient traditions and spiritual insights—provides a profound understanding of the cosmic influences that shape our destiny. However, for many, this ancient wisdom often feels complex and difficult to grasp.

"Easy Astrology: Learn in Simple Steps" was born out of my passion for simplifying this profound knowledge and making it accessible to everyone. I realized that while there is a growing interest in Vedic Astrology, there is also a need for a structured and easy-to-follow guide that breaks down its principles practically and engagingly.

In this book, I have carefully designed a step-by-step approach that introduces you to the core concepts of Vedic Astrology—covering the fundamentals of planetary positions, zodiac signs, birth charts, and the intricate connections between cosmic energy and human life. Whether you are a beginner eager to explore astrology or someone looking to deepen your knowledge, this book will provide you with the tools and confidence to interpret astrological charts and apply this wisdom to your own life.

Throughout this journey, my goal has been to demystify astrology, remove unnecessary jargon, and present information in a way that is both easy to understand and enjoyable to explore. I believe that understanding the cosmic blueprint can empower us to make better decisions, align with our life's purpose, and cultivate harmony in our relationships.

As you embark on this exciting exploration, I encourage you to approach it with an open heart and a curious mind. May this book serve as a guiding light, helping you unlock the secrets of Vedic Astrology and uncover the hidden patterns that shape your life.

CONTENTS

About the Author   3

Foreword   5

Chapter 1 Introduction to Vedic Astrology   11
- What is Vedic Astrology?   11
- 1 B) Difference Between Vedic and Western Astrology   13
- 1 C) Importance of Astrology in Daily Life   15
- 1 D) How is Astrology Based on Planetary Movements?   16

Chapter 2 2A) The 12 Zodiac Signs (Rashis) – Characteristics
           of Each Sign   18
- 2 B) The 9 Planets (Navagrahas) – Their Effects and
  Significance   21
- 2 C) The 12 Houses (Bhavas) – Their Meanings in
  a Horoscope   25
- 2 C) The 27 Nakshatras in Vedic Astrology
  (Lunar Mansions) – Role of Constellations   30

Chapter 3 The Birth Chart (Kundli) Explained   61
- 3 A) How a Birth Chart (Janma Kundali) is Created   61
- 3 B) Role of Date, Time, and Place of Birth in Creating
  a Birth Chart (Janma Kundali)   63
- 3 C) Difference Between Lagna (Ascendant) and Moon
  Sign (Chandra Rashi)   65

Chapter 4 Understanding Planetary Aspects and Conjunctions   76

• 4 A) How Planets Influence Each Other   76

• 4 B) Benefic vs. Malefic Planets in Vedic Astrology   80

• 4 C) What Are Yogas in Vedic Astrology?   85

Chapter 5 The Dasha System (Planetary Periods) in Vedic Astrology   114

• What is the Vimshottari Dasha System?   114

• How Planetary Periods Affect Life Events   115

Chapter 6 Transit (Gochar) and Its Effects in Astrology   119

Chapter 7 Basic Predictions Using a Birth Chart   134

• Introduction to the Birth Chart   134

• Planets and Their Predictive Meaning   134

• Signs and How Energy Is Expressed   135

• Houses – Areas of Life Impacted   136

• Aspects – Planetary Interactions   137

• Making Basic Predictions + Transits   138

• Importance of Lagna and Moon Sign for Analysis   138

• Checking Career, Marriage and Health from a Horoscope   141

• Under standing the Frame work – The Houses and Planets Involved   142

• Career – Profession, Success and Direction   142

• Marriage – Relationships, Love, and Compatability   143

• Health – Vitality, Illness and Recovery   144

• Integrating Career, Marriage and Health _ A Holistic Approach   146

Chapter 8 Remedies in Vedic Astrology   147

Conclusion: Your Journey Through the Stars ✳   *155*

References   *157*

Disclaimer   *159*

CHAPTER 1

INTRODUCTION TO VEDIC ASTROLOGY

What is Vedic Astrology?

Vedic Astrology, also known as **Jyotish Shastra**, is an ancient system of astrology that originated in India over **5,000 years ago**. It is based on the **Vedas**, the oldest sacred texts of Hinduism. Vedic astrology is used to analyze a person's life, predict future events, and understand karmic influences.

Key Features of Vedic Astrology

1. **Based on the Sidereal Zodiac (Fixed Star System)**

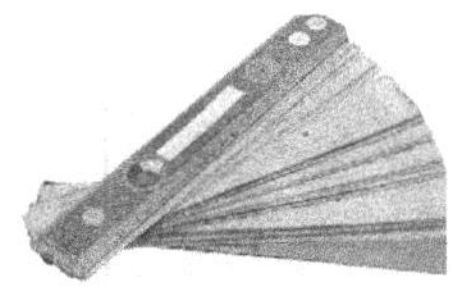

   - Unlike Western astrology (which uses the Tropical Zodiac), Vedic astrology follows the **Sidereal Zodiac**, which is aligned with the actual constellations in the sky.

   - This means that many people have a different Sun sign in Vedic astrology compared to Western astrology.

2. **Importance of the Moon Sign (Rashi) and Ascendant (Lagna)**

   - In Vedic astrology, more importance is given to the **Moon sign (Rashi)** and **Ascendant (Lagna)** rather than just the Sun sign.

   - The Moon sign represents emotions and mental state, while the Ascendant represents personality and life path.

3. Use of the 9 Planets (Navagrahas)

- Vedic astrology considers **nine planets (Navagrahas):**

    - **Sun (Surya)** – Soul, authority, ego

    - **Moon (Chandra)** – Mind, emotions, mother

    - **Mars (Mangal)** – Energy, courage, aggression

    - **Mercury (Budh)** – Intelligence, communication, business

    - **Jupiter (Guru)** – Wisdom, growth, prosperity

    - **Venus (Shukra)** – Love, beauty, luxury

    - **Saturn (Shani)** – Discipline, karma, hardships

    - **Rahu (North Node)** – Ambitions, desires, illusions

    - **Ketu (South Node)** – Spirituality, detachment, past karma

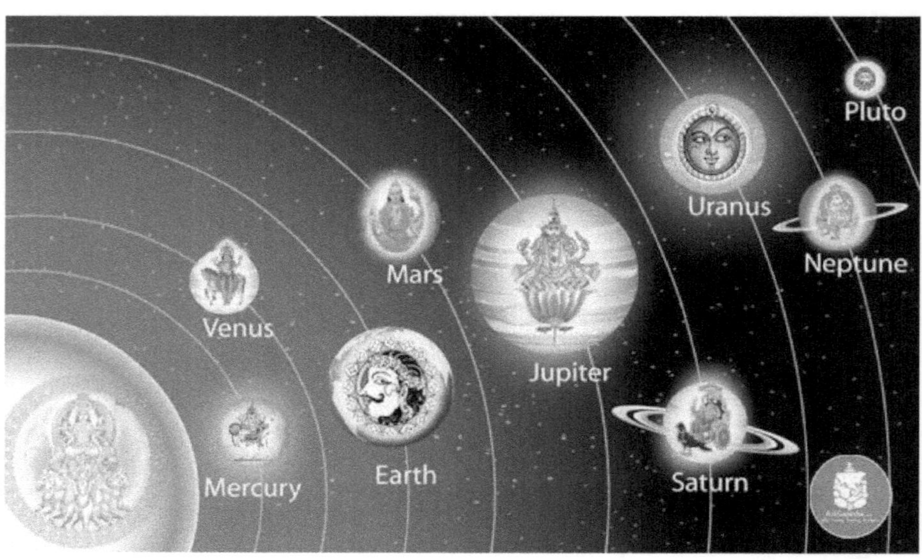

4. 12 Houses (Bhavas) and Their Significance

- The birth chart (Kundli) is divided into **12 houses**, each representing different aspects of life, such as personality, wealth, career, marriage, health, etc.

5. **27 Nakshatras (Lunar Constellations)**

   - The Moon moves through **27 Nakshatras**, which further refine predictions. Each Nakshatra has a ruling planet and unique characteristics.

6. **The Dasha System (Planetary Time Periods)**

   - Vedic astrology has a system called **Vimshottari Dasha**, which divides life into different planetary periods. Each planet rules for a specific number of years, influencing life events.

7. **Transit (Gochar) Analysis**

   - The movement of planets (transits) affects a person's life in different ways. The transit of **Saturn (Shani)** and **Jupiter (Guru)** is particularly important for long-term effects.

8. **Karma and Free Will**

   - Vedic astrology is based on the principle of **karma** (past actions influencing present life).

   - However, it also allows for **free will** and suggests remedies like **mantras, gemstones, rituals, and charity** to reduce negative influences.

1 B) Difference Between Vedic and Western Astrology

Astrology is an ancient practice used to understand human life and destiny based on planetary movements. **Vedic Astrology (Jyotish)** and **Western Astrology** are the two most popular systems, but they differ in various aspects.

1. **Basis of Calculation**

   - **Vedic Astrology**: Uses the **Sidereal Zodiac**, which considers the actual positions of stars and constellations.

   - **Western Astrology**: Uses the **Tropical Zodiac**, which is based on the Earth's seasons and does not account for the shifting position of stars over time.

2. **Zodiac System**

   ○ **Vedic:** Uses the **fixed** or "nakshatra-based" zodiac (Sidereal).

   ○ **Western:** Uses the **moving** or season-based zodiac (Tropical).

3. **Planets Considered**

   ○ **Vedic:** Considers 9 planets (Navagrahas) – Sun, Moon, Mars, Mercury, Jupiter, Venus, Saturn, Rahu, and Ketu.

   ○ **Western:** Considers 10 planets – Sun, Moon, Mercury, Venus, Mars, Jupiter, Saturn, Uranus, Neptune, and Pluto.

4. **Focus and Purpose**

   ○ **Vedic:** More predictive and focuses on **karma, destiny, and remedies** to improve life.

   ○ **Western:** More psychological, focusing on **personality traits, emotions, and self-awareness**.

5. **Divisional Charts**

   ○ **Vedic:** Uses **many divisional charts (Vargas)** like Navamsa and Dasamsa for detailed analysis.

   ○ **Western:** Primarily relies on the **birth chart (natal chart)** without divisional charts.

6. **Dashas (Timing System)**

   ○ **Vedic:** Uses **Dasha systems** (e.g., Vimshottari Dasha) to predict events accurately.

   ○ **Western:** Uses **progressions and transits** to predict events.

7. **Aspects and Houses**

* **Vedic:** Has **12 houses** and uses **full, half, and special planetary aspects**.

* **Western:** Also has **12 houses**, but aspects are based on geometric angles (e.g., conjunctions, oppositions, trines).

8. **Remedies**

   ○ **Vedic**: Provides remedies like **gemstones, mantras, pujas, donations, and fasting**.

   ○ **Western**: Focuses on **self-awareness, psychological healing, and meditation**.

✨ Conclusion

- **Vedic Astrology** is **more predictive, detailed, and karma-based**.

- **Western Astrology** is **psychological, personality-focused, and season-based**.

Both systems have their strengths and are widely used depending on cultural and personal preferences. ✨

1 C) Importance of Astrology in Daily Life

Astrology plays a significant role in daily life by helping people understand their personality, future possibilities, and life decisions. It is based on planetary movements and their influence on human life.

✨ How does Astrology Help in Daily Life?

1. **Self-Understanding** – Helps in knowing strengths, weaknesses, and personality traits.

2. **Career Guidance** – Suggest suitable career paths and work opportunities.

3. **Relationship Compatibility** – Assists in understanding love and marriage compatibility.

4. **Health Predictions** – Warns about possible health issues and suggests remedies.

5. **Financial Planning** – Helps in making better financial decisions.

6. **Timing Important Events** – Guides in choosing the right time for marriage, job changes, or investments.

7. **Stress Management** – Provides mental peace by offering remedies like meditation, mantras, and pujas.

✨ Conclusion

Astrology is a guiding tool that helps people make informed decisions and lead a balanced life. While not a substitute for hard work and effort, it provides insights that can improve daily living. 🌙🌑

1 D) How is Astrology Based on Planetary Movements?

Astrology is the study of how planets, the Sun, and the Moon influence human life. The movement of these celestial bodies through different zodiac signs affects personality, emotions, and future events.

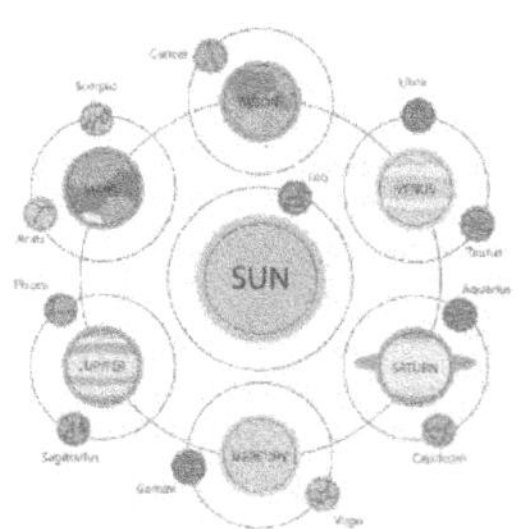

🌏 Key Points:

1. **Zodiac System** – The sky is divided into 12 zodiac signs, and planets move through them, influencing different aspects of life.

2. **Planetary Positions** – At the time of birth, the position of planets forms a unique **birth chart (horoscope)** that determines a person's traits and life path.

3. **Transits & Dashas** – As planets move, they bring life changes (good or bad), depending on their position.

4. **Effects on Life** – Each planet rules specific areas like career (Saturn), love (Venus), wisdom (Jupiter), and emotions (Moon).

5. **Predicting Future Events** – Astrologers analyze planetary movements to predict opportunities and challenges and suggest remedies.

 **Conclusion**

Astrology is deeply connected to planetary movements. It helps us understand life events, make better decisions, and prepare for the future.

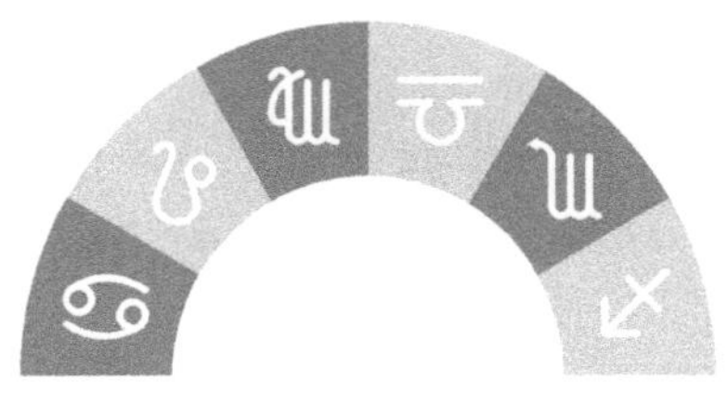

CHAPTER 2

2A) The 12 Zodiac Signs (Rashis) – Characteristics of Each Sign

Each zodiac sign (Rashi) has unique traits that influence a person's personality, behavior, and destiny. Here's a brief overview of all 12 signs:

1. Mesha Rashi (Aries) – The Warrior

- **Element:** Fire
- **Ruling Planet:** Mars (Mangal)
- **Traits:** Bold, energetic, leadership qualities, adventurous, impatient
- **Strengths:** Courageous, confident, determined
- **Weaknesses:** Short-tempered, impulsive

2. Vrishabha Rashi (Taurus) – The Reliable One

- **Element:** Earth
- **Ruling Planet:** Venus (Shukra)
- **Traits:** Practical, loyal, patient, loves comfort
- **Strengths:** Hardworking, dependable, artistic
- **Weaknesses:** Stubborn, materialistic

♊ 3. Mithuna Rashi (Gemini) – The Communicator

- **Element:** Air 
- **Ruling Planet:** Mercury (Budh)
- **Traits:** Intelligent, social, curious, witty
- **Strengths:** Adaptable, quick learner, expressive
- **Weaknesses:** Moody, indecisive

♋ 4. Karka Rashi (Cancer) – The Nurturer

- **Element:** Water 
- **Ruling Planet:** Moon (Chandra)
- **Traits:** Emotional, caring, family-oriented, intuitive
- **Strengths:** Loyal, protective, empathetic
- **Weaknesses:** Moody, sensitive, insecure

♌ 5. Simha Rashi (Leo) – The Leader

- **Element:** Fire 
- **Ruling Planet:** Sun (Surya)
- **Traits:** Charismatic, ambitious, confident, loves attention
- **Strengths:** Brave, generous, creative
- **Weaknesses:** Egoistic, dominating

♍ 6. Kanya Rashi (Virgo) – The Perfectionist

- **Element:** Earth 
- **Ruling Planet:** Mercury (Budh)
- **Traits:** Practical, detail-oriented, intelligent, hardworking

- ○ **Strengths:** Analytical, organized, and dedicated
- ○ **Weaknesses:** Overcritical, perfectionist, anxious

7. Tula Rashi (Libra) – The Diplomat

- ○ **Element:** Air 
- ○ **Ruling Planet:** Venus (Shukra)
- ○ **Traits:** Peace-loving, charming, fair-minded, artistic
- ○ **Strengths:** Balanced, social, cooperative
- ○ **Weaknesses:** Indecisive, avoids confrontations

8. Vrischika Rashi (Scorpio) – The Intense One

- ○ **Element:** Water 
- ○ **Ruling Planet:** Mars (Mangal)
- ○ **Traits:** Passionate, secretive, determined, powerful
- ○ **Strengths:** Strong-willed, resourceful, loyal
- ○ **Weaknesses:** Jealous, possessive, stubborn

9. Dhanu Rashi (Sagittarius) – The Explorer

- ○ **Element:** Fire 
- ○ **Ruling Planet:** Jupiter (Guru)
- ○ **Traits:** Adventurous, optimistic, philosophical, loves freedom
- ○ **Strengths:** Honest, independent, enthusiastic
- ○ **Weaknesses:** Impulsive, impatient, tactless

10. Makara Rashi (Capricorn) – The Hard Worker

- ○ **Element:** Earth
- ○ **Ruling Planet:** Saturn (Shani)

- o **Traits:** Disciplined, practical, responsible, career-focused
- o **Strengths:** Determined, ambitious, patient
- o **Weaknesses:** Rigid, workaholic, pessimistic

 11. Kumbha Rashi (Aquarius) – The Visionary

- o **Element:** Air 
- o **Ruling Planet:** Saturn (Shani)
- o **Traits:** Independent, creative, humanitarian, free-spirited
- o **Strengths:** Intelligent, innovative, progressive
- o **Weaknesses:** Unpredictable, detached, rebellious

12. Meena Rashi (Pisces) – The Dreamer

- o **Element:** Water
- o **Ruling Planet:** Jupiter (Guru)
- o **Traits:** Sensitive, artistic, intuitive, spiritual
- o **Strengths:** compassion, imaginative, selfless
- o **Weaknesses:** Escapist, overly emotional, and indecisive

 Conclusion

Each zodiac sign has its strengths and challenges. Understanding them helps in personal growth, relationships, and life decisions.

2 B) The 9 Planets (Navagrahas) – Their Effects and Significance

The **Nava grahas** (nine celestial bodies) in Vedic astrology play a crucial role in shaping human life and destiny. These planets influence different aspects of a person's health, career, relationships, and spirituality. Below is an overview of the **Nava grahas, their significance, and their effects:**

1. **Sun (Surya) – The King of Planets**

   - **Significance**: Represents power, authority, health, and vitality.

   - **Effects**: A strong Sun brings success, confidence, and leadership, while a weak Sun can cause ego issues, health problems, and career struggles.

   - **Associated Zodiac**: Leo (Simha)

   - **Day**: Sunday

2. **Moon (Chandra) – The Mind and Emotions**

   - **Significance**: It governs emotions, intuition, mental peace, and the subconscious mind.

   - **Effects**: A well-placed Moon grants emotional stability and creativity, whereas a weak Moon can lead to mood swings, anxiety, and indecisiveness.

   - **Associated Zodiac**: Cancer (Karka)

   - **Day**: Monday

3. **Mars (Mangal) – The Warrior Planet**

   - **Significance**: Represents courage, energy, aggression, and discipline.

   - **Effects**: A strong Mars gives determination and success in sports and leadership, but an afflicted Mars can lead to anger issues, conflicts, and accidents.

   - **Associated Zodiac**: Aries (Mesha) and Scorpio (Vrishchika)

- **Day**: Tuesday

4. Mercury (Budha) – The Planet of Communication

- o **Significance**: Governs intelligence, communication, business, and analytical ability.

- o **Effects**: A strong Mercury enhances speech, intellect, and financial success, while a weak Mercury causes misunderstandings, nervous disorders, and financial losses.

- o **Associated Zodiac**: Gemini (Mithuna) and Virgo (Kanya)

- • **Day**: Wednesday

5. Jupiter (Guru) – The Planet of Wisdom

- o **Significance**: It represents knowledge, wisdom, spirituality, and prosperity.

- o **Effects**: A well-placed Jupiter brings good fortune, success, and spiritual growth, while a weak Jupiter can lead to financial struggles and a lack of direction.

- o **Associated Zodiac**: Sagittarius (Dhanu) and Pisces (Meena)

- o **Day**: Thursday

6. Venus (Shukra) – The Planet of Love and Luxury

- o **Significance**: Governs relationships, beauty, luxury, art, and pleasures.

- o **Effects**: A strong Venus enhances love life, creativity, and wealth, while an afflicted Venus can cause relationship problems and financial losses.

- o **Associated Zodiac**: Taurus (Vrishabha) and Libra (Tula)

- o **Day**: Friday

7. **Saturn (Shani) – The Lord of Karma**

- ○ **Significance**: It represents discipline, patience, hardships, and justice.

- ○ **Effects**: A strong Saturn rewards hard work with success, but a weak or afflicted Saturn can bring obstacles, delays, and suffering.

- ○ **Associated Zodiac**: Capricorn (Makara) and Aquarius (Kumbha)

- ○ **Day**: Saturday

8. **Rahu – The Shadow Planet (North Node of the Moon)**

- ○ **Significance**: Governs desires, illusions, technology, and unconventional paths.

- ○ **Effects**: A strong Rahu grants fame and success in unusual fields, while an afflicted Rahu causes confusion, addictions, and legal troubles.

- ○ **No specific Zodiac ownership**

- ○ **Day**: Saturday or Wednesday (Varies by belief)

9. **Ketu – The Spiritual Planet (South Node of the Moon)**

- ○ **Significance**: Represents detachment, past karma, and spiritual growth.

- ○ **Effects**: A well-placed Ketu enhances spiritual wisdom and intuition, while an afflicted Ketu leads to confusion, sudden losses, and instability.

- ○ **No specific Zodiac ownership**

- ○ **Day**: Tuesday or Thursday (Varies by belief)

❖ Conclusion

The Navagrahas influence every aspect of life. Their placement in the birth chart determines challenges and opportunities. Remedies such as chanting mantras, wearing gemstones, and performing rituals can help balance their effects. Understanding their significance can help individuals make informed life choices and overcome difficulties.

2 C) The 12 Houses (Bhavas) – Their Meanings in a Horoscope

Pisces Jupiter	Aries Mars	Taurus Venus	Gemini Mercury
Aquarius Saturn			Cancer Moon
Capricorn Saturn			Leo Sun
Sagittarius Jupiter	Scorpio Mars	Libra Venus	Virgo Mercury

In **Vedic astrology**, the **12 houses (Bhavas)** in a birth chart (Kundali) represent different aspects of life. Each house is ruled by a specific zodiac sign and has unique significations that shape an individual's personality, career, relationships, and destiny. Below is a detailed explanation of the **12 houses and their meanings**:

1st House – The House of Self (Lagna / Ascendant)

- **Significance**: Represents physical appearance, personality, health, and overall life path.
- **Effects:** A strong 1st house gives confidence, success, and good health, while a weak 1st house can lead to self-doubt and health issues.

- **Planetary Association**: Sun (Surya) does well here.

- **Zodiac Connection**: Aries (Mesha) is the natural ruler.

2nd House – The House of Wealth and Speech

- **Significance**: Governs wealth, family, speech, savings, food habits, and values.

- **Effects**: A well-placed 2nd house brings financial stability and good communication skills, whereas an afflicted 2nd house can lead to financial struggles and speech issues.

- **Planetary Association**: Jupiter (Guru) gives prosperity here.

- **Zodiac Connection**: Taurus (Vrishabha) is the natural ruler.

3rd House – The House of Courage and Siblings

- **Significance**: Represents communication, courage, younger siblings, short journeys, skills, and determination.

- **Effects**: A strong 3rd house brings confidence and success in media, writing, and sports, while a weak one may cause fearfulness and strained sibling relationships.

- **Planetary Association**: Mars (Mangal) is strong here.

- **Zodiac Connection**: Gemini (Mithuna) is the natural ruler.

4th House – The House of Home and Comfort

- **Significance**: Represents mother, home, property, vehicles, emotions, inner peace, and childhood.

- **Effects**: A well-placed 4th house ensures happiness in domestic life, real estate gains, and emotional security, while a weak 4th house may lead to family disputes and instability.

- **Planetary Association**: Moon (Chandra) is favorable here.

- **Zodiac Connection**: Cancer (Karka) is the natural ruler.

5ᵗʰ House – The House of Creativity and Children

- **Significance**: It governs intelligence, creativity, romance, children, education, and speculation (like stock markets).

- **Effects**: A strong 5ᵗʰ house brings academic success, love, and artistic skills, while an afflicted one can cause difficulties in education and relationships.

- **Planetary Association**: Sun (Surya) is powerful here.

- **Zodiac Connection**: Leo (Simha) is the natural ruler.

6ᵗʰ House – The House of Health and Enemies

- **Significance**: Represents health, enemies, debts, competition, legal matters, and obstacles.

- **Effects**: A strong 6ᵗʰ house helps in overcoming enemies, maintaining good health, and succeeding in competitive fields, whereas a weak 6ᵗʰ house can lead to health issues and financial burdens.

- **Planetary Association**: Mercury (Budha) is beneficial here.

- **Zodiac Connection**: Virgo (Kanya) is the natural ruler.

7ᵗʰ House – The House of Partnerships and Marriage

- **Significance**: It governs marriage, business partnerships, spouse, legal contracts, and public dealings.

- **Effects**: A well-placed 7ᵗʰ house ensures a harmonious marriage and successful business partnerships, while an afflicted one can cause delays in marriage and relationship issues.

- **Planetary Association**: Venus (Shukra) flourishes here.

- **Zodiac Connection**: Libra (Tula) is the natural ruler.

8ᵗʰ House – The House of Transformation and Secrets

- **Significance**: Represents longevity, hidden knowledge, inheritance, accidents, transformations, and occult sciences.

- **Effects**: A strong 8th house gives deep intuition, resilience, and spiritual growth, while a weak one can bring sudden losses, accidents, and psychological stress.

- **Planetary Association**: Saturn (Shani) is significant here.

- **Zodiac Connection**: Scorpio (Vrishchika) is the natural ruler.

9th House – The House of Fortune and Spirituality

- **Significance**: Represents luck, dharma (righteousness), long-distance travel, higher education, philosophy, and religion.

- **Effects**: A strong 9th house brings good fortune, success in higher studies, and spiritual progress, whereas a weak one can lead to a lack of faith and struggles in education.

- **Planetary Association**: Jupiter (Guru) is at its best here.

- **Zodiac Connection**: Sagittarius (Dhanu) is the natural ruler.

10th House – The House of Career and Public Life

- **Significance**: Governs career, profession, reputation, authority, and achievements.

- **Effects**: A well-placed 10th house leads to success in career, fame, and recognition, while an afflicted one can cause career instability and loss of status.

- **Planetary Association**: Saturn (Shani) strengthens professional life here.

- **Zodiac Connection**: Capricorn (Makara) is the natural ruler.

11th House – The House of Gains and Desires

- **Significance**: Represents income, achievements, social networks, aspirations, and elder siblings.

- **Effects**: A strong 11th house ensures financial success and fulfillment of desires, while a weak one can bring missed opportunities and financial instability.

- **Planetary Association**: Jupiter (Guru) favors wealth here.

- **Zodiac Connection**: Aquarius (Kumbha) is the natural ruler.

12th House – The House of Liberation and Losses

- **Significance**: It governs spirituality, foreign travel, expenditures, isolation, and the subconscious mind.

- **Effects**: A well-placed 12th house brings spiritual enlightenment and success in foreign lands, while an afflicted one may cause financial losses, loneliness, or hospitalization.

- **Planetary Association**: Ketu and Saturn work well here.

- **Zodiac Connection**: Pisces (Meena) is the natural ruler.

✸ Conclusion

Each house in astrology plays a crucial role in determining different aspects of life. The influence of **planets (Grahas)** in these houses further refines their effects. A deeper understanding of the **12 houses** helps in analyzing an individual's strengths, challenges, and life path.

#12 **Vyaya Bhava** Losses, Donations, Imprisonment, Sacrifice, Moksha	**#1** **Tanu Bhava** Self, Physical Body, Longevity & General Characteristics	**#2** **Dhana Bhava** Wealth / Money, Resources, Family, Speech	**#3** **Bhratra Bhava** Siblings, Courage, Bravery, Initiatives, Communication
#11 **Labha Bhava** Gains, Profits, Friends, Elder Brother	**Bhava Chakra**		**#4** **Sukha Bhava** Mother, Peace, Happiness, Education, Heart
#10 **Karma Bhava** Work, Career, Profession, Activities in Society			**#5** **Suta Bhava** Children, Fame, Talents & Skills, Emotions, Intelligence
#9 **Bhagya Bhava** Father, Luck, Fortunes, Guru / Teacher, Dharma, Character	**#8** **Mrityu Bhava** Longevity, Inheritence, Troubles, Worries, Secrets	**#7** **Jaya Bhava** Spouse, Desires, Partners in Business, Death	**#6** **Shatru Bhava** Enemies, Obstacles, Diseases, Accidents

2 C) The 27 Nakshatras in Vedic Astrology (Lunar Mansions) – Role of Constellations

Nakshatras, also known as **Lunar Mansions**, are 27 divisions of the sky, each covering **13° 20'** of the zodiac. They are an essential part of Vedic astrology and are closely linked to the **Moon's movement** through the zodiac. Each Nakshatra has unique characteristics, ruling planets, deities, and symbolism that influence a person's nature, destiny, and life path.

List of 27 Nakshatras & Their Detailed Meanings

1. Ashwini Nakshatra (0°00' - 13°20' Aries)

- **Symbol: Horse's head**
- **Deity: Ashwini Kumars (Celestial Twin Healers)**
- **Ruling Planet: Ketu**
- **Nature: Swift, energetic, pioneering**
- **Guna: Rajas**
- **Animal: Male Horse**
- **Dosha: Vata**
- **Meaning: Speed, healing, new beginnings**

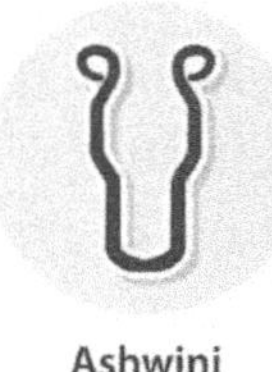

Ashwini

Key Characteristics

- **Fast-moving and dynamic: Always eager to start new projects.**
- **Excellent healers: Natural ability to heal others physically and emotionally.**
- **Youthful and energetic: Vibrant, charming, and full of life.**
- **Adventurous: Love challenges and exploration.**
- **Highly intelligent and innovative: Great at problem-solving.**

Professions & Career Paths

- **Doctors, healers, surgeons**
- **Athletes, sports professionals**

- Military personnel, police, firefighters

- Entrepreneurs, innovators

Challenges

- Restless and impatient.

- Difficulty in completing tasks before starting new ones.

Favorable Activities

- Starting new ventures.

- Healing, medical work, and therapy.

- Travel and adventure activities.

2. Bharani Nakshatra (13°20' - 26°40' Aries)

- Symbol: Yoni (Female reproductive organ)

- Deity: Yama (God of Death & Justice)

- Ruling Planet: Venus

- Nature: Transformative, passionate, intense

- Guna: Rajas

- Animal: Male Elephant

- Dosha: Pitta

- Meaning: Creation, destruction, rebirth

Bharani

Key Characteristics

- Highly passionate and intense: Deep emotions and strong willpower.

- Creative and artistic: Drawn to beauty, music, and design.

- Transformational personalities: They go through major life changes.

- Good at handling responsibility: Reliable and trustworthy.

Professions & Career Paths

- Artists, musicians, dancers
- Lawyers, judges, administrators
- Entrepreneurs, business owners
- Psychologists, counselors

Challenges

- Can be overly stubborn or aggressive.
- May experience emotional ups and downs.

Favorable Activities

- Engaging in artistic and creative pursuits.
- Taking on leadership and management roles.

3. Krittika Nakshatra (26°40' Aries - 10°00' Taurus)

- Symbol: Razor or Knife
- Deity: Agni (Fire God)
- Ruling Planet: Sun
- Nature: Fierce, strong-willed, sharp intellect

Krittika

- Guna: Rajas
- Animal: Female Goat
- Dosha: Pitta
- Meaning: Purification, cutting through illusions

Key Characteristics

- Strong-willed and determined: Once they decide something, they achieve it.
- Powerful and courageous: Fearless in facing challenges.

- Sharp intelligence: Quick learners with deep insight.

- Leadership skills: Natural ability to guide others.

Professions & Career Paths

- Military personnel, police officers

- Surgeons, butchers, metalworkers

- Politicians, leaders, managers

- Scientists, researchers

Challenges

- Can be overly aggressive or confrontational.

- Prone to being too critical of others.

Favorable Activities

- Taking leadership roles.

- Pursuing intellectual and research-based work.

- Engaging in self-discipline and personal transformation.

4. Rohini Nakshatra (10°00' - 23°20' Taurus)

- Symbol: Chariot or Ox Cart

- Deity: Brahma (Creator God)

- Ruling Planet: Moon

- Nature: Creative, sensual, materialistic

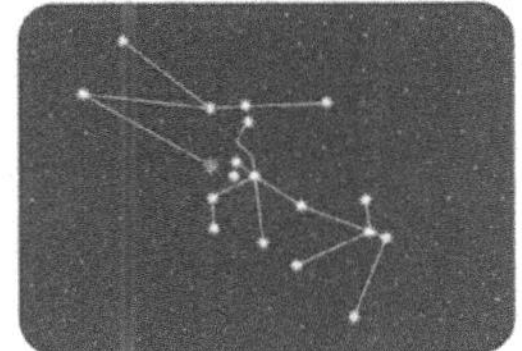

Rohini

- Guna: Rajas

- Animal: Male Cobra

- Dosha: Kapha

- Meaning: Growth, fertility, beauty

Key Characteristics

- Highly attractive and charismatic: Draws people in with charm.

- Strong love for beauty and luxury: Appreciates art, music, and fashion.

- Emotionally deep and sensitive: Forms strong relationships.

- Highly creative and imaginative: Artistic and innovative thinkers.

Professions & Career Paths

- Fashion designers, artists, musicians

- Real estate professionals, architects

- Business owners, agriculturalists

- Models, actors, public figures

Challenges

- Tendency to become materialistic or overly indulgent.

- Can be emotionally possessive.

Favorable Activities

- Engaging in creative arts and business ventures.

- Enjoying relationships and social gatherings.

5. Mrigashira Nakshatra (23°20' Taurus - 6°40' Gemini)

- Symbol: Deer's Head

- Deity: Soma (Moon God)

- Ruling Planet: Mars

- Nature: Curious, restless, intellectual

- Guna: Tamas

Mrigashirsha

- Animal: Female Snake

- Dosha: Vata

- Meaning: Searching, seeking, curiosity

Key Characteristics

- Curious and explorative: Loves to learn and discover new things.

- Fast learners and good communicators: Intelligent and witty.

- Restless and always in search of something: Dislike being tied down.

- Romantic and charming: Attracts others easily.

Professions & Career Paths

- Journalists, writers, researchers

- Salespeople, marketing experts

- Travelers, tour guides, explorers

- Poets, actors, performers

Challenges

- Can struggle with focus and commitment.

- Prone to overthinking and worry.

Favorable Activities

- Learning new skills and pursuing education.

- Traveling and exploring different cultures.

6. Ardra Nakshatra (6°40' - 20°00' Gemini)

- Symbol: Teardrop, Diamond

- Deity: Rudra (Storm God)

- Ruling Planet: Rahu

- Nature: Intense, transformative, emotional

- Guna: Tamas

- Animal: Female Dog

- Dosha: Vata

- Meaning: Destruction, renewal, inner strength

Ardra

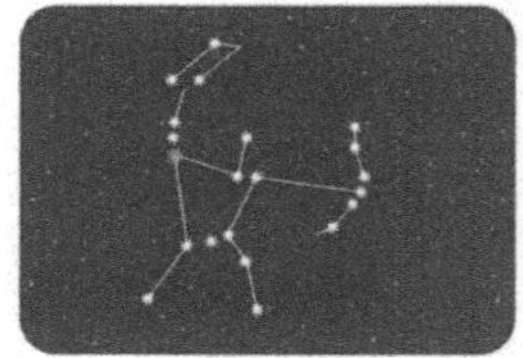

Key Characteristics

- Intense and emotional: Deep thinkers with strong emotions.

- Strong desire for change: Attracted to transformation.

- Highly intelligent and analytical: Good at research and problem-solving.

- Can endure hardships: Resilient and adaptable.

Professions & Career Paths

- Scientists, researchers, psychologists

- Surgeons, medical professionals

- Crisis managers, revolutionaries

- Writers, poets, philosophers

Challenges

- Prone to mood swings and emotional upheavals.

- May experience sudden life changes.

Favorable Activities

- Engaging in deep study and research.

- Transformative spiritual practices.

7. Punarvasu Nakshatra (20°00' Gemini - 3°20' Cancer)

- Symbol: Bow & Quiver

- Deity: Aditi (Mother of the Gods)

- **Ruling Planet: Jupiter**

- **Nature: Wise, nurturing, optimistic**

- **Guna: Sattva**

- **Animal: Female Cat**

- **Dosha: Kapha**

- **Meaning: Renewal, second chances, adaptability**

Punarvasu

Key Characteristics

- **Positive and optimistic: Always sees the brighter side of life.**

- **Loving and nurturing: Takes care of others.**

- **Highly intelligent and philosophical: Enjoys deep thinking.**

- **Adventurous and open-minded: Loves travel and new experiences.**

Professions & Career Paths

- **Writers, teachers, philosophers**

- **Travelers, spiritual seekers**

- **Entrepreneurs, business leaders**

Challenges

- **Can be indecisive and scattered.**

- **May struggle with sticking to one thing for long.**

Favorable Activities

- **Engaging in teaching and writing.**

- **Traveling and exploring new cultures**

8. Pushya Nakshatra (3°20' - 16°40' Cancer)

- **Symbol: Lotus, Cow's Udder**

- **Deity: Brihaspati (Jupiter – Guru of the Gods)**

- **Ruling Planet:** Saturn
- **Nature:** Nourishing, disciplined, spiritual
- **Guna:** Sattva
- **Animal:** Male Sheep
- **Dosha:** Kapha
- **Meaning:** Prosperity, growth, nourishment

Pushya

Key Characteristics

- **Kind and generous:** Pushya natives are nurturing and protective.
- **Highly disciplined and responsible:** They work hard and stay committed.
- **Spiritual seekers:** Drawn to religious and ethical teachings.
- **Respected in society:** Their wisdom and guidance are valued.

Professions & Career Paths

- Priests, teachers, spiritual leaders
- Social workers, caregivers, medical professionals
- Businesspeople, administrators
- Farmers, dairy-related industries
  Challenges
- May struggle with emotional expression.
- Can be too rigid or overly traditional.

Favorable Activities

- Engaging in teaching and mentoring.
- Pursuing religious or spiritual studies.
- Financial investments and wealth-building.

9. Ashlesha Nakshatra (16°40' - 30°00' Cancer)

- Symbol: Serpent

- Deity: Naga (Serpent Deities)

- Ruling Planet: Mercury

- Nature: Mysterious, hypnotic, cunning

- Guna: Tamas

- Animal: Male Cat

- Dosha: Pitta

- Meaning: Secret knowledge, transformation, depth

Ashlesha

Key Characteristics

- Intelligent and sharp-minded: Ashlesha natives are strategic thinkers.

- Hypnotic and persuasive: They can influence and manipulate others.

- Secretive and private: They keep their thoughts and plans hidden.

- Emotionally intense: They experience deep emotions but don't express them openly.

Professions & Career Paths

- Psychologists, therapists, astrologers

- Politicians, intelligence officers, spies

- Lawyers, negotiators, business strategists

- Researchers, scientists, geneticists

Challenges

- Can be overly secretive and distrusting.

- Prone to manipulation or deception.

Favorable Activities

- Engaging in deep research and strategy.
- Exploring occult sciences and mysticism.
- Practicing self-discipline and self-awareness.

10. Magha Nakshatra (0°00' - 13°20' Leo)

- **Symbol:** Royal Throne
- **Deity:** Pitris (Ancestors)
- **Ruling Planet:** Ketu
- **Nature:** Proud, traditional, authoritative
- **Guna:** Tamas
- **Animal:** Male Rat
- **Dosha:** Kappa
- **Meaning:** Heritage, honor, tradition

Magha

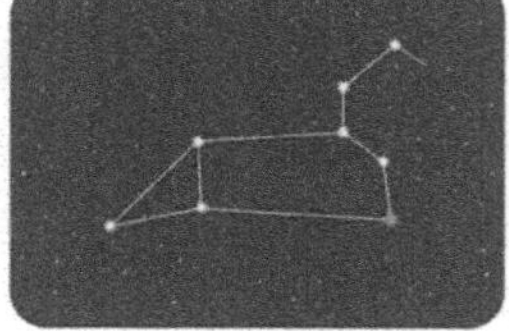

Key Characteristics

- **Proud and authoritative:** Magha natives have strong leadership qualities.
- **Deeply connected to ancestry:** They value traditions and heritage.
- **Enjoy positions of power:** They seek respect and status in society.
- **Protective and responsible:** They guide and mentor others.

Professions & Career Paths

- Politicians, leaders, government officials
- Historians, genealogists, museum curators
- Military officers, security personnel
- Spiritual guides, mentors

Challenges

- Can be egoistic or too attached to status.
- Struggles with change and flexibility.

Favorable Activities

- Performing rituals and honoring ancestors.
- Taking leadership and management roles.
- Building a strong personal and professional legacy.

11. Purva Phalguni Nakshatra (13°20' - 26°40' Leo)

- **Symbol: Hammock, Front Legs of a Bed**
- **Deity: Bhaga (God of Wealth and Fortune)**
- **Ruling Planet: Venus**
- **Nature: Romantic, luxurious, artistic**
- **Guna: Rajas**
- **Animal: Male Rat**
- **Dosha: Vata**
- **Meaning: Pleasure, prosperity, enjoyment**

Purva Phalguni

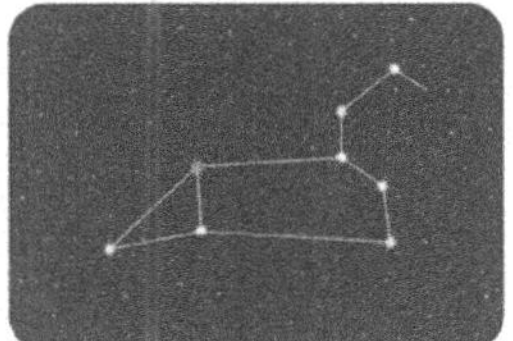

Key Characteristics

- **Lovers of luxury and beauty: Purva Phalguni natives enjoy life's pleasures.**
- **Charming and attractive: They have magnetic personalities.**
- **Creative and expressive: They excel in arts, music, and drama.**
- **Relaxed and easy-going: They enjoy comfort and leisure.**

Professions & Career Paths

- **Artists, actors, models, entertainers**
- **Fashion designers, interior decorators**

- Entrepreneurs in luxury goods and services

- Event planners, relationship coaches
    Challenges

- Can become too indulgent or lazy.

- Struggles with discipline and responsibility.

Favorable Activities

- Socializing, romance, and entertainment.

- Pursuing artistic and creative projects.

- Engaging in self-care and relaxation.

12. Uttara Phalguni Nakshatra (26°40' Leo - 10°00' Virgo)

- Symbol: Bed, Marriage Cot

- Deity: Aryaman (God of Contracts and Unions)

- Ruling Planet: Sun

- Nature: Dutiful, responsible, ethical

- Guna: Rajas

- Animal: Female Cow

- Dosha: Pitta

- Meaning: Commitment, duty, agreements

Uttara Phalguni

Key Characteristics

- Highly responsible and ethical: They follow strong moral values.

- Commitment-oriented: Excellent in partnerships and marriage.

- Good leadership abilities: Capable of managing large projects.

- Supportive and helpful: They assist and uplift others.

Professions & Career Paths

- Lawyers, contract managers, diplomats

- Teachers, social reformers, humanitarians

- Business executives, administrators

- Marriage counselors, relationship advisors

Challenges

- Can be overly rigid in their beliefs.

- May struggle with personal relationships due to high expectations.
  Favorable Activities

- Legal agreements, marriage, and business partnerships.

- Engaging in social service and charity work.

13. Hasta Nakshatra (10°00' - 23°20' Virgo)

- Symbol: Hand or Palm

- Deity: Savitar (Sun God)

- Ruling Planet: Moon

- Nature: Skillful, hardworking, dexterous

Hasta

- Guna: Sattva

- Animal: Male Buffalo

- Dosha: Vata

- Meaning: Skill, craftsmanship, manual work

Key Characteristics

- Excellent with hands-on work: Skilled in craftsmanship and manual labor.

- Clever and intelligent: Quick thinkers and problem-solvers.

- Persuasive and charming: Good at influencing people.

- Hardworking and dedicated: Committed to their goals.

Professions & Career Paths

- Artisans, craftsmen, musicians

- Surgeons, massage therapists, healers

- Magicians, illusionists, performers

- Businesspeople, sales representatives

Challenges

- Can be overly critical or perfectionist.

- May struggle with patience.

Favorable Activities

- Hand-based skills and professions.

- Business and negotiations.

- Learning new crafts and talents.

14. Chitra Nakshatra (23°20' Virgo - 6°40' Libra)

- Symbol: Bright Jewel

- Deity: Vishwakarma (Celestial Architect)

- Ruling Planet: Mars

- Nature: Creative, ambitious, dynamic

- Guna: Tamas

- Animal: Female Tiger

Chitra

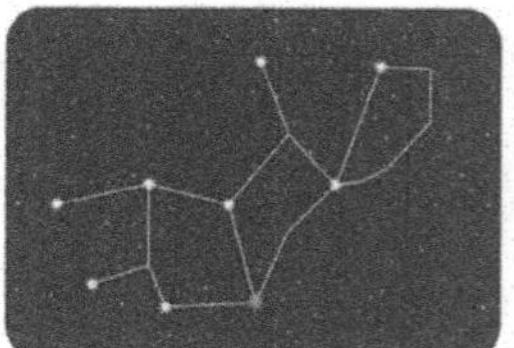

- Dosha: Pitta

- Meaning: Beauty, craftsmanship, brilliance

Key Characteristics

- **Highly creative and artistic: Skilled in design, art, and architecture.**

- **Hardworking and ambitious: Determined to create something meaningful.**

- **Charismatic and attractive: Draws attention effortlessly.**

15. Swati (6°40' - 20°00' Libra)

- **Symbol:** Young sprout swaying in the wind

- **Deity:** Vayu (God of Wind)

- **Ruling Planet:** Rahu

- **Nature:** Independent, adaptable, free-spirited

- **Guna:** Tamas

- **Animal:** Male Buffalo

- **Dosha:** Kapha

- **Meaning:** Freedom, movement, independence

Swati

Key Characteristics

- **Highly independent:** They love freedom and dislike restrictions.

- **Great adaptability:** Like the wind, they can adjust to any situation.

- **Persuasive speakers:** Good at influencing others.

- **Business-oriented:** Strong entrepreneurial and negotiation skills.

- **Restless and exploratory:** They enjoy travel and new experiences.

Professions & Career Paths

- Businesspeople, traders, diplomats

- Travelers, pilots, transport workers

- Public speakers, motivational coaches
- Spiritual seekers, philosophers

Challenges

- Struggles with commitment in relationships.
- May be overly ambitious, leading to dissatisfaction.

Favorable Activities

- Business deals, networking, and partnerships.
- Traveling, learning new skills, and self-improvement.

16. Vishakha (20°00' Libra - 3°20' Scorpio)

- **Symbol:** Archway with a decorated pot
- **Deity:** Indra & Agni (Gods of Power and Fire)
- **Ruling Planet:** Jupiter
- **Nature:** Goal-oriented, determined, competitive
- **Guna:** Sattva
- **Animal:** Male Tiger
- **Dosha:** Pitta
- **Meaning:** Success, achievement, focus

Vishakha

Key Characteristics

- **Highly ambitious:** They are focused on achieving goals.
- **Strong willpower:** They do not give up easily.
- **Magnetic personality:** They attract people with their charm.
- **Dual nature:** Torn between materialism and spirituality.

Professions & Career Paths

- Politicians, lawyers, activists
- Athletes, warriors, military leaders

- Business executives, CEOs

- Teachers, philosophers

Challenges

- May be too aggressive in pursuing success.

- Prone to power struggles and conflicts.

Favorable Activities

- Starting new ventures and projects.

- Setting long-term goals and working toward them.

17. Anuradha (3°20' - 16°40' Scorpio)

- **Symbol:** Lotus flower

- **Deity:** Mitra (God of Friendship)

- **Ruling Planet:** Saturn

- **Nature:** Loyal, disciplined, cooperative

- **Guna:** Sattva

- **Animal:** Female Deer

- **Dosha:** Vata

- **Meaning:** Friendship, devotion, discipline

Anuradha

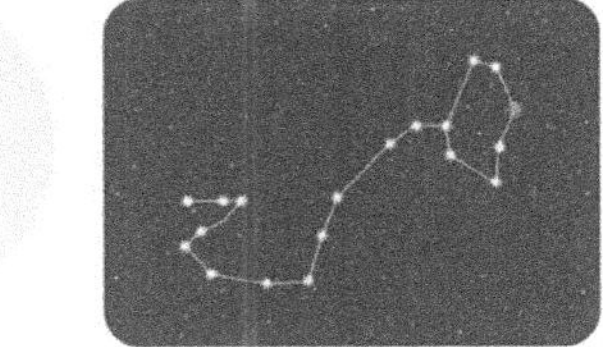

Key Characteristics

- **Loyal and trustworthy:** Excellent friends and partners.

- **Disciplined:** Hardworking and responsible.

- **Spiritual seekers:** They have deep philosophical minds.

- **Good teamwork skills:** They work well in groups.

Professions & Career Paths

- Diplomats, negotiators, managers

- Researchers, scientists, psychologists

- Spiritual teachers, philosophers

- Musicians, artists

Challenges

- Tendency to overwork and neglect personal life.

- May struggle with emotional vulnerability.

Favorable Activities

- Forming partnerships and making alliances.

- Spiritual activities, meditation, and self-improvement.

18. Jyeshtha (16°40' - 30°00' Scorpio)

- **Symbol:** Circular earring or umbrella

- **Deity:** Indra (King of Gods)

Jyestha

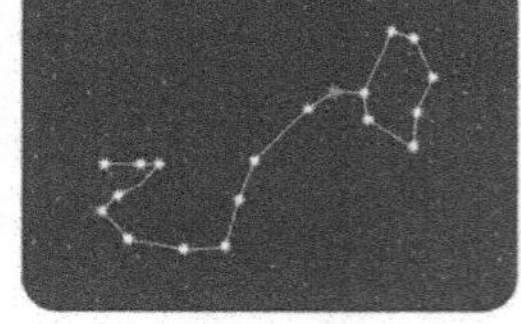

- **Ruling Planet:** Mercury

- **Nature:** Protective, authoritative, strategic

- **Guna:** Sattva

- **Animal:** Male Deer

- **Dosha:** Pitta

- **Meaning:** Seniority, leadership, wisdom

Key Characteristics

- **Natural leaders:** They take charge in difficult situations.

- **Strong sense of responsibility:** They protect and guide others.

- **Powerful intuition:** They have deep insights and wisdom.

- **Secretive:** They keep their emotions and thoughts private.

Professions & Career Paths

- Military leaders, police officers, politicians

- CEOs, managers, executives

- Spiritual leaders, counselors, psychologists

- Secret agents, intelligence officers

Challenges

- Can be controlling or dominating.

- Struggles with trust issues.

Favorable Activities

- Leadership roles and decision-making.

- Taking on challenges that require strategy and intelligence.

19. Mula (0°00' - 13°20' Sagittarius)

- **Symbol:** A tied bunch of roots

- **Deity:** Nirriti (Goddess of Destruction)

- **Ruling Planet:** Ketu

- **Nature:** Transformative, mystical, intense

- **Guna:** Tamas

- **Animal:** Male Dog

- **Dosha:** Vata

- **Meaning:** Roots, transformation, destruction for renewal

Mula

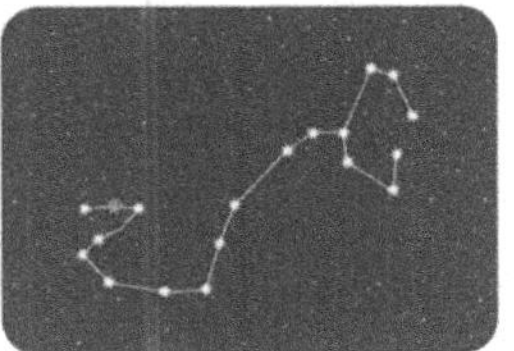

Key Characteristics

- **Seekers of truth:** They explore deep spiritual and philosophical topics.

- **Transformative personalities:** They undergo major life changes.

- **Rebellious and unconventional:** They dislike authority and restrictions.

- **Highly intelligent and intuitive:** They understand hidden knowledge.

Professions & Career Paths

- Scientists, researchers, philosophers
- Psychologists, astrologers, spiritual healers
- Detectives, investigators, forensic experts
- Revolutionaries, reformers

Challenges

- May face sudden upheavals and crises in life.
- Can be overly detached or aloof.

Favorable Activities

- Meditation, self-reflection, and spiritual practices.
- Research and deep study of hidden knowledge.

20. Purva Ashadha (13°20' - 26°40' Sagittarius)

- **Symbol:** Elephant's tusk, fan
- **Deity:** Apas (Goddess of Water)
- **Ruling Planet:** Venus
- **Nature:** Confident, persuasive, optimistic
- **Guna:** Rajas
- **Animal:** Male Monkey
- **Dosha:** Pitta
- **Meaning:** Victory, invincibility, self-confidence

Purva Ashadha

Key Characteristics

- **Highly determined:** They do not give up easily.
- **Excellent communicators:** They persuade others with ease.

- **Charming and attractive:** People are drawn to them.
- **Strong leadership abilities:** They inspire and motivate others.

Professions & Career Paths

- Public speakers, teachers, politicians
- Salespeople, marketing executives, business leaders
- Writers, journalists, artists
- Lawyers, diplomats

Challenges

- Can become overly proud or arrogant.
- Struggles with stubbornness and ego.

Favorable Activities

- Leadership roles and competitive activities.
- Public speaking, negotiations, and teaching.

✥ Conclusion

These **six Nakshatras (Swati to Purva Ashadha)** represent a powerful mix of **independence, ambition, wisdom, transformation, and leadership.** Each Nakshatra has unique strengths and challenges, influencing personality, career, and relationships.

21. Uttara Ashadha Nakshatra (26°40' Sagittarius - 10°00' Capricorn)

- **Symbol:** Elephant's tusk, planks of a bed
- **Deity:** Vishwadevas (Universal Gods)
- **Ruling Planet:** Sun ☉
- **Nature:** Righteous, determined, disciplined
- **Guna:** Sattva

Uttara Ashadha

- **Animal:** Male Mongoose (rare in Nakshatra symbolism)
- **Dosha:** Vata
- **Meaning:** Unchallengeable victory, leadership, perseverance

Key Characteristics

- **Determined and ambitious:** They have strong willpower and do not give up easily.
- **Highly responsible:** They carry out their duties with honour and discipline.
- **Righteous and moral:** They value justice and truth.
- **Natural leaders:** They often take authoritative positions in society.

Professions & Career Paths

- Government officials, politicians, law enforcers
- Judges, social reformers, teachers
- Military personnel, leaders, entrepreneurs
- Philosophers, researchers, diplomats

Challenges

- Can be too rigid or inflexible.
- Might struggle with emotional expression.

Favorable Activities

- Leadership roles, government work, legal affairs.
- Taking on responsibilities that require long-term commitment.

22. Shravana Nakshatra (10°00' - 23°20' Capricorn)

- **Symbol:** Ear, Three Footsteps
- **Deity:** Vishnu (The Preserver)
- **Ruling Planet:** Moon ☽

- **Nature:** Wise, intellectual, observant
- **Guna:** Rajas
- **Animal:** Male Monkey
- **Dosha:** Kapha
- **Meaning:** Listening, wisdom, learning

Shravana

Key Characteristics

- **Highly intellectual:** Excellent learners with great memory.
- **Good communicators:** Skilled in speech, writing, and negotiation.
- **Spiritual and wise:** Have a deep connection to religious or philosophical teachings.
- **Seekers of knowledge:** They love acquiring and sharing wisdom.

Professions & Career Paths

- Teachers, professors, authors
- Spiritual leaders, counselors, mentors
- Public speakers, media personalities
- Diplomats, interpreters, journalists

Challenges

- Can be overly talkative or overly secretive.
- Might struggle with making quick decisions.

Favorable Activities

- Studying, teaching, and engaging in discussions.
- Spiritual practices, listening to elders and wise individuals.

23. Dhanishta Nakshatra (23°20' Capricorn - 6°40' Aquarius)

- **Symbol:** Drum, Flute

- **Deity:** Eight Vasus (Gods of Abundance & Light)

- **Ruling Planet:** Mars ♂

- **Nature:** Ambitious, energetic, musical

- **Guna:** Tamas

- **Animal:** Female Lion

- **Dosha:** Pitta

- **Meaning:** Fame, wealth, rhythm

Dhanishtha

Key Characteristics

- **Ambitious and hardworking:** Strive for success and recognition.

- **Musically inclined:** Many musicians, artists, and performers belong to this Nakshatra.

- **Generous and kind-hearted:** They help others when in a position of power.

- **Good with finances:** They understand wealth creation and business.

Professions & Career Paths

- Musicians, dancers, performers

- Businesspeople, financial experts, wealth managers

- Politicians, public figures, celebrities

- Athletes, defense personnel

Challenges

- Can be arrogant or overly status-conscious.

- Might struggle with maintaining personal relationships due to career focus.

Favorable Activities

- Engaging in creative arts, music, and performances.

- Financial planning, investments, and wealth-building.

24. Shatabhisha Nakshatra (6°40' - 20°00' Aquarius)

- **Symbol:** Circle, 100 Flowers or Stars

- **Deity:** Varuna (God of Cosmic Waters)

- **Ruling Planet:** Rahu ☊

- **Nature:** Secretive, independent, scientific

- **Guna:** Tamas

- **Animal:** Female Horse

- **Dosha:** Vata

- **Meaning:** Healing, mystery, knowledge

Shatabhisha

Key Characteristics

- **Deep thinkers and researchers:** Love uncovering hidden truths.

- **Interested in medicine and healing:** Many doctors and healers belong to this Nakshatra.

- **Mysterious and secretive:** Prefer solitude and working behind the scenes.

- **Innovative and futuristic:** Good at thinking outside the box.

Professions & Career Paths

- Scientists, researchers, astrologers

- Doctors, alternative healers, psychologists

- Technologists, inventors, IT experts

- Detectives, spies, forensic analysts

Challenges

- Can be reclusive or detached from society.

- Struggles with emotional vulnerability.

Favorable Activities

- Research, scientific discoveries, medical work.

- Deep spiritual and mystical studies.

25. Purva Bhadrapada Nakshatra (20°00' Aquarius - 3°20' Pisces)

- **Symbol:** Two Front Legs of a Funeral Cot

- **Deity:** Aja Ekapada (One-Footed Serpent God)

- **Ruling Planet:** Jupiter ♃

- **Nature:** Intense, mysterious, revolutionary

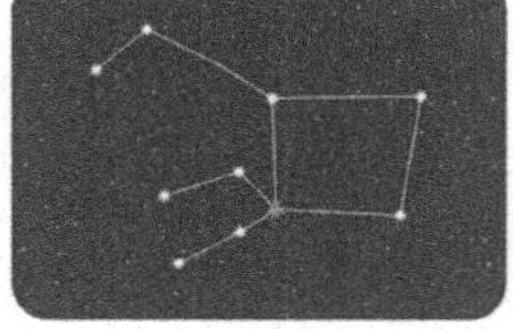

Purva Bhadrapada

- **Guna:** Sattva

- **Animal:** Male Lion

- **Dosha:** Vata

- **Meaning:** Transformation, fire, purification

Key Characteristics

- **Highly spiritual and philosophical:** Deep thinkers who question life's meaning.

- **Intense and unpredictable:** Can be drawn to extreme beliefs or actions.

- **Have a strong moral compass:** Stand up for justice and righteousness.

- **Capable of deep transformation:** Their lives go through major changes.

Professions & Career Paths

- Spiritual leaders, yogis, monks

- Scientists, researchers, inventors

- Activists, revolutionaries, motivational speakers

- Writers, poets, artists

Challenges

- Prone to extreme thinking or radical views.

- Can be overly serious and intense.

Favorable Activities

- Engaging in deep philosophical and spiritual studies.

- Fighting for justice and transformation in society.

26. Uttara Bhadrapada Nakshatra (3°20' - 16°40' Pisces)

- **Symbol:** Two Back Legs of a Funeral Cot

- **Deity:** Ahir Budhnya (Serpent of the Depths)

- **Ruling Planet:** Saturn ♄

- **Nature:** Wise, patient, philosophical

- **Guna:** Tamas

- **Animal:** Female Cow

- **Dosha:** Pitta

- **Meaning:** Stability, wisdom, deep knowledge

Uttara Bhadrapada

Key Characteristics

- **Highly patient and disciplined:** They take a long-term approach to life.

- **Deeply wise and knowledgeable:** Good at giving advice and guiding others.

- **Spiritual seekers:** Interested in enlightenment and the mysteries of life.

Professions & Career Paths

- Teachers, professors, scholars

- Spiritual gurus, monks, meditators

- Scientists, philosophers, psychologists

- Writers, journalists, publishers

Challenges

- Can be too detached or withdrawn.

- Struggles with practical decision-making.

Favorable Activities

- Spiritual and meditation practices.

- Engaging in deep research and writing.

27. Revati (रेवती) – "The Wealthy and Prosperous One"

Sanskrit Meaning: "The Wealthy One" or "The Nourisher"

Symbol: A drum, a fish

Deity: Pushan (The Nourisher and Protector, a form of the Sun)

Revati

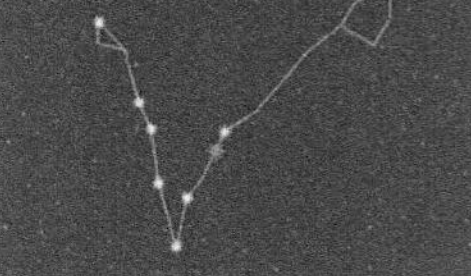

Ruling Planet: Mercury (Budha)

Element: Ether (Akasha)

Animal Symbol: Female Elephant

Nature (Guna): Sattva – Sattva – Sattva

Dosha: Kapha (Watery)

Key Characteristics:

- **Gentle, kind-hearted, and generous**
- **Highly intuitive, creative, and artistic**
- **Deeply compassionate, loving, and selfless**
- **Strong connection to higher realms and spiritual wisdom**
- **Often dreamy and imaginative, with a love for fantasy and storytelling**

Positive Traits:

- ☑ **Highly creative and artistic**
- ☑ **Deeply spiritual and intuitive**
- ☑ **Strong sense of compassion and empathy**
- ☑ **Can achieve great success through persistence**
- ☑ **Natural protectors and caregivers**

Negative Traits:

- ✕ **Can be overly idealistic or naive**
- ✕ **Prone to escapism or avoiding harsh realities**
- ✕ **Can be emotionally vulnerable and sensitive**
- ✕ **May struggle with indecisiveness**

Professions & Career Fields:

- **Musicians, artists, writers, poets**
- **Psychologists, healers, spiritual guides**
- **Marine-related jobs, shipping industry**
- **Humanitarian work, social services**

Health Issues:

- **Nervous system disorders**
- **Anxiety, depression, or mental health issues**
- **Sleep disorders or lack of proper rest**

Nakshatras			Nakshatras Head	Dasha Period
Ashwini	Magha	Mula	Ketu	7 Years
Bharani	Purva	Purva Ashadha	Venus	20 Years
Krittika	Uttara	Uttara Ashadha	Sun	6 Years
Rohini	Hasta	Shravana	Moon	10 Years
Mrigashirsha	Chitra	Dhanishtha	Mars	7 Years
Ardra	Swati	Shatabhisha	Rahu	18 Years
Punarvasu	Vishakha	Purva bhadra	Jupiter	16 Years
pushyami	Anuradha	Uttara Bhadra	Saturn	19 Years
Ashlesha	Jyestha	Revati	Mercury	17 Years

<table>
<tr>
<td>

Purva bhadra - $3^0 20'$
Uttara Bhadra - $13^0 20'$
Revati   - $13^0 20'$
————
$30^0 00'$

</td>
<td>

Ashwini - $13^0 20'$
Bharani - $13^0 20'$
Krittika - $3^0 20'$
————
$30^0 00'$

</td>
<td>

Krittika   - $10^0 00'$
Rohini   - $13^0 20'$
Mrigashirsha- $6^0 40'$
————
$30^0 00'$

</td>
<td>

Mrigashirsha - $6^0 40'$
Ardra   - $13^0 20'$
Punarvasu   - $10^0 00'$
————
$30^0 00'$

</td>
</tr>
<tr>
<td>

Dhanishtha   - $6^0 40'$
Shatabhisha - $13^0 20'$
Purva bhadra - $10^0 00'$
————
$30^0 00'$

</td>
<td colspan="2" rowspan="2"></td>
<td>

Punarvasu - $3^0 20'$
Pushyami - $13^0 20'$
Ashlesha - $13^0 20'$
————
$30^0 00'$

</td>
</tr>
<tr>
<td>

Uttara Ashadha - $10^0 00'$
Shravana   - $13^0 20'$
Dhanishtha   - $6^0 40'$
————
$30^0 00'$

</td>
<td>

Magha   - $13^0 20'$
Purva   - $13^0 20'$
Uttara   - $3^0 20'$
————
$30^0 00'$

</td>
</tr>
<tr>
<td>

Mula   - $13^0 20'$
Purva Ashadha - $13^0 20'$
Uttara Ashadha - $3^0 20'$
————
$30^0 00'$

</td>
<td>

Vishakha - $3^0 20'$
Anuradha - $13^0 20'$
Jyestha   - $13^0 20'$
————
$30^0 00'$

</td>
<td>

Chitra   - $6^0 40'$
Swati   - $13^0 20'$
Vishakha - $10^0 00'$
————
$30^0 00'$

</td>
<td>

Uttara   - $10^0 00'$
Hasta   - $13^0 20'$
Chitra   - $6^0 40'$
————
$30^0 00'$

</td>
</tr>
</table>

CHAPTER 3

The Birth Chart (Kundli) Explained

3 A) How a Birth Chart (Janma Kundali) is Created

A Janma Kundali (Birth Chart) is a detailed map of the sky at the exact moment and location of a person's birth. It is a crucial tool in Vedic astrology and is used to analyse personality, predict life events, and understand karmic influences. Here's a step-by-step breakdown of how it is created:

1. Collecting Birth Details

To create an accurate birth chart, three key details are required:

- Date of Birth (Tithi) – The exact date when the person was born.

- Time of Birth – The precise time of birth (hours, minutes, and if possible, seconds). Even a small difference in time can change planetary positions.

- Place of Birth – The latitude and longitude of the birth location are needed to determine the planetary positions accurately.

2. Calculating the Planetary Positions

Using the birth details, astrologers refer to Panchang (Hindu almanac) or use modern astrology software to determine:

- The positions of the nine planets (Navagrahas) – Sun, Moon, Mars, Mercury, Jupiter, Venus, Saturn, Rahu, and Ketu.

- The Ascendant (Lagna/Rising Sign) – The zodiac sign that was rising on the eastern horizon at the time of birth.

- The 12 Houses (Bhavas) – These represent different aspects of life (career, relationships, health, etc.).

- The Nakshatra (Lunar Mansion) – The constellation in which the Moon was located at birth.

3. Constructing the Birth Chart

A Janma Kundali is a 12-house chart, usually drawn in one of these formats:

- North Indian Style (diamond-shaped houses)

- South Indian Style (rectangular houses)

- East Indian Style (square-based system)

Each house represents a different area of life, and planets placed within them influence different aspects of a person's destiny.

4. Analyzing the Charts

Once the Kundali is created, astrologers interpret it by examining:

- The placement and strength of planets in different houses.

- The influence of Dasha (planetary periods) and Gochar (transits).

- The impact of aspects (drishti) and yogas (planetary combinations) that bring positive or negative results.

5. Using Astrology Software for Accuracy

Today, astrologers use advanced software like Jagannatha Hora, Kundli, or AstroSage to generate precise birth charts within seconds. These tools incorporate astronomical calculations to provide accurate predictions.

✨ Conclusion

A Janma Kundali is a powerful tool in astrology that helps understand a person's strengths, challenges, and life path. It serves as a cosmic blueprint, guiding individuals based on the planetary influences at the time of their birth.

3 B) Role of Date, Time, and Place of Birth in Creating a Birth Chart (Janma Kundali)

A **Janma Kundali (Birth Chart)** is a unique astrological blueprint of an individual's life, based on the exact positions of celestial bodies at the time of birth. The three essential details—**Date, Time, and Place of Birth**—play a crucial role in determining an accurate birth chart.

1. Role of Date of Birth

The **date of birth** helps determine:

- The **Sun Sign (Surya Rashi)** – The zodiac sign where the Sun was positioned on that particular day.
- The **Lunar Month and Tithi** – Important in Vedic astrology, these determine spiritual and karmic influences.
- The **Planetary Positions** – The approximate placement of planets (like Mars, Jupiter, and Venus) on the given date.

☞ Why It Matters:

The date of birth provides the base positions of celestial bodies, helping to shape an individual's basic characteristics and long-term planetary cycles.

2. Role of Time of Birth

The **exact time of birth** is crucial for:

- **Ascendant (Lagna or Rising Sign)** – This changes roughly every **two hours** and determines the **first house** of the birth chart, affecting personality, health, and life path.

- **Moon Sign (Chandra Rashi)** – The Moon moves quickly through the zodiac, and its placement influences emotions, mental state, and behavior.

- **Planetary Houses (Bhavas)** – The time of birth determines in which houses the planets are placed, influencing different areas of life (career, marriage, wealth, etc.).

👉 **Why It Matters:**

Even a **5-minute difference** in birth time can change the Lagna, altering predictions significantly. If the exact birth time is unknown, rectification techniques are used to estimate it.

3. Role of Place of Birth

The **geographical location** (latitude and longitude) of birth affects:

- **The Ascendant Calculation** – The Lagna changes based on the observer's location on Earth.

- **Planetary Positions in the Sky** – The visible position of planets varies depending on where someone is born.

- **Time Zone Adjustments** – Astrology charts use **Local Mean Time (LMT)** to adjust planetary placements correctly.

👉 **Why It Matters:**

Two people born on the **same date and time but in different locations** will have different Lagnas and house placements, leading to unique destinies.

3 C) Difference Between Lagna (Ascendant) and Moon Sign (Chandra Rashi)

In Vedic astrology, **Lagna (Ascendant)** and **Moon Sign (Chandra Rashi)** are two crucial elements of a birth chart, each playing a unique role in shaping an individual's personality, emotions, and life experiences.

1. What is Lagna (Ascendant)?

The **Lagna (Ascendant)** is the zodiac sign that was **rising on the eastern horizon** at the exact moment and place of birth. It represents the **first house (Tanu Bhava)** in the birth chart and is considered the starting point of one's life journey.

Key Aspects of Lagna:

✓ **Represents:** Physical body, personality, outward appearance, and first impressions.

✓ **Determined by:** The **exact time and place of birth** (changes approximately every 2 hours).

✓ **Influence:** Governs how a person interacts with the world and their overall approach to life.

✓ **Long-term Impact:** Affects one's destiny, health, and how external circumstances unfold over time.

Example: If someone has Aries (Mesha) as their Lagna, they are likely to be energetic, bold, and action-oriented.

How to Calculate Ascendant (Lagna) in Birth Chart

Detailed Lagna (Ascendant) Calculation in Astrology

The Lagna (Ascendant) is the zodiac sign that was rising on the eastern horizon at the exact time and location of birth. It is the most crucial point in a birth chart as it influences a person's personality, physical appearance, and overall life path.

This guide will explain the detailed step-by-step process to calculate the Lagna manually.

Step 1: Collecting Birth Data

To accurately determine the Lagna, you need the following details:

1. Date of Birth (DOB) – Example: *15ᵗʰ August 1995*

2. Time of Birth (TOB) – Example: *12:30 PM*

3. Place of Birth (POB) – Example: *Hyderabad, India*

   ○ This is required to determine latitude and longitude.

   ○ Hyderabad: Latitude: 17.385° N, Longitude: 78.486° E

Step 2: Convert Birth Time to Greenwich Mean Time (GMT)

Since planetary and sidereal time tables are based on GMT (Greenwich Mean Time), we must adjust for the time zone difference.

1. Check the Time Zone of Birthplace:

   ○ India Standard Time (IST) = GMT +5:30

   ○ If the birth time is 12:30 PM IST, subtract 5 hours 30 minutes to get GMT

   ○ 12:30 PM IST - 5:30 = 7:00 AM GMT

Now, the Universal Time (UT) of birth is 7:00 AM.

Step 3: Calculate Greenwich Sidereal Time (GST)

Sidereal Time is the time based on the Earth's rotation relative to the fixed stars rather than the Sun.

1. Find GST at Midnight for the Given Date

   ○ The Greenwich Sidereal Time (GST) at 0:00 GMT (midnight) can be found using an ephemeris or an online tool.

   ○ Let's assume for *15ᵗʰ August 1995*, GST at 00:00 GMT = 10h 50m

2. **Adjust for Birth Time**

   - Add the time elapsed since midnight (7:00 AM GMT) in sidereal time.

   - 7 hours in Sidereal Time = (7×1.0027379) = 7.019 hours

   - So, GST at birth time = 10h 50m + 7h 1m = 17h 51m

Step 4: Convert GST to Local Sidereal Time (LST)

Now, adjust for the longitude of the birth location.

1. **Convert Longitude to Time**

   - **Longitude of Hyderabad = 78.486° E**

   - **Each degree of longitude corresponds to 4 minutes of time.**

   - **78.486° × 4 min = 313.94 minutes = 5 hours 13 minutes**

2. **Adjust GST for Longitude**

   - **If longitude is East, add the time. If West, subtract.**

   - **LST = 17h 51m + 5h 13m = 23h 04m**

Thus, Local Sidereal Time (LST) = 23 hours 4 minutes.

Step 5: Determine the Ascendant (Lagna Sign)

1. **Divide the 24-hour Sidereal Day into 12 Zodiac Signs**

   - **Each sign rises for approximately 2 hours, but this varies slightly due to Earth's axial tilt.**

2. **Check Which Sign is Rising at LST**

   - **Reference an Ascendant Table or a software to find the sign that was rising at LST 23:04.**

   - **At 23:04 LST, the Ascendant falls in Aries (Mesha Lagna).**

   - **To get the exact degree of the Ascendant, use an astrological table or software.**

Step 6: Verify and Refine the Degree of the Ascendant

To find the exact degree of the Lagna, follow these steps:

1. Each zodiac sign spans 30 degrees and stays on the eastern horizon for roughly 2 hours.

2. Using the calculated LST (23:04), you can interpolate the degree of the rising sign using software or an ephemeris.

3. If using software, enter the birth details, and it will provide the exact Ascendant degree (e.g., *Aries 12°14'*).

Example Calculation Summary

- Date of Birth: 15th August 1995

- Time of Birth: 12:30 PM IST

- Place of Birth: Hyderabad, India

- Time Zone: GMT +5:30

- Converted GMT Birth Time: 7:00 AM

- GST at Midnight: 10:50 AM

- Adjusted GST at Birth Time: 17:51

- Local Sidereal Time (LST): 23:04

- Rising Sign (Lagna): Aries (Mesha Lagna)

Thus, the Lagna for this birth chart is Aries at approximately 12 degrees.

Alternative: Using Astrology Software for Quick Calculation

Instead of manual calculation, you can use astrology software or websites like:

- Jagannatha Hora (JHora)

- AstroSage.com

- **Drik Panchang**

- **Parashara's Light**

These tools automatically compute the Lagna based on birth details.

🎇 Conclusion

- **The Lagna (Ascendant) is the most critical point in a horoscope.**

- **It depends on the exact time and location of birth.**

- **Using the sidereal time method, we determine which zodiac sign was rising at the eastern horizon.**

- **This method ensures precise calculations and is used in Vedic astrology for birth chart analysis.**

Would you like me to calculate the Lagna for a specific birth chart? 🚀

2. What is Moon Sign (Chandra Rashi)?

The **Moon Sign** is the zodiac sign in which the **Moon** was positioned at the time of birth. It represents the **mind, emotions, instincts, and inner self**.

Key Aspects of Moon Sign:

✓ **Represents:** Emotions, subconscious mind, mental state, and inner personality.

✓ **Determined by:** The **Moon's position** in a particular zodiac sign (changes approximately every 2.5 days).

✓ **Influence:** Governs feelings, reactions, and how a person processes emotions.

✓ **Short-term Impact:** Affects mood swings, intuition, and emotional responses.

Example: If someone has their Moon in Cancer (Karka Rashi), they may be deeply emotional, intuitive, and family-oriented.

3. Major Differences Between Lagna and Moon Sign

Feature	Lagna (Ascendant)	Moon Sign (Chandra Rashi)
What it Represents	Outer personality, physical body, and life path	Inner emotions, subconscious mind, and instincts
Determined By	The zodiac sign rising on the eastern horizon at birth	The zodiac sign where the Moon is placed at birth
Changes Every	~2 hours	~2.5 days
Role in Astrology	Defines overall personality, health, and destiny	Governs emotional nature, mental strength, and intuition
Influences	Long-term life path and major events	Emotional responses and day-to-day feelings
Importance in Horoscope	Used to create the **Lagna Chart (D-1)**	Used for **mental compatibility and daily predictions**

4. Which One is More Important?

◈ **For External Life & Destiny** → **Lagna is crucial** as it shapes personality, career, and overall path in life.

◈ **For Emotions & Mental State** → **Moon Sign is vital** because it affects feelings, relationships, and decision-making.

📌 In Vedic astrology, **both Lagna and Moon Sign are equally important**, but their roles are different. A strong Lagna ensures stability in life, while a well-placed Moon brings emotional strength and peace of mind.

1. Impact of Each Planet's Placement

☼ Sun (Surya) – Soul, Authority, Ego

Strong Sun (Exalted in Aries, Own Sign in Leo):

✔ Natural leadership qualities, high confidence, good health.

✔ Success in government, politics, or leadership roles.

✓ Strong willpower and good decision-making skills.

Weak Sun (Debilitated in Libra, Afflicted by Malefic Planets):

✗ Low self-esteem, health issues, struggles in career.

✗ Conflicts with father or authority figures.

✗ Lack of recognition in professional life.

☽ **Moon (Chandra) – Emotions, Mind, Mother**

Strong Moon (Exalted in Taurus, Own Sign in Cancer):

✓ Emotional stability, intuition, caring nature.

✓ Strong mental health and inner peace.

✓ Good relationship with mother and family.

Weak Moon (Debilitated in Scorpio, Afflicted by Malefics):

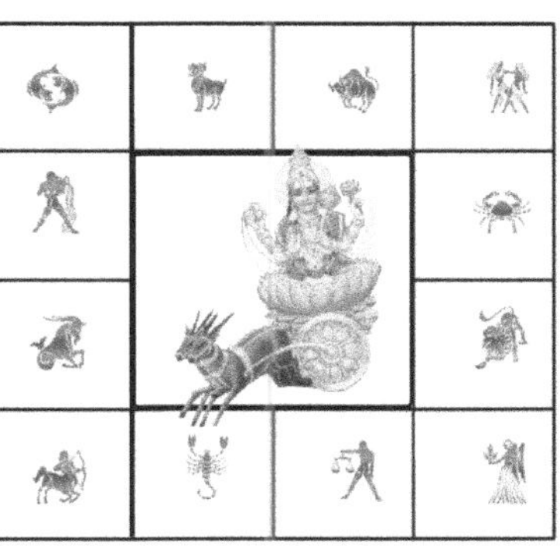

✗ Mood swings, anxiety, emotional instability.

✗ Difficulties in handling stress and relationships.

✗ Lack of mental peace and disturbances in personal life.

🜨 **Mars (Mangal) – Energy, Courage, Action**

Strong Mars (Exalted in Capricorn, Own Sign in Aries/Scorpio):

✓ Courageous, ambitious, physically strong.

✓ Good leadership and success in competitive fields (sports, military, engineering).

✓ Ability to take risks and overcome obstacles.

Weak Mars (Debilitated in Cancer, Afflicted by Malefics):

✗ Aggression, anger issues, impulsiveness.

✗ Conflicts in relationships, problems in marriage (Manglik Dosha).

✗ Accidents, injuries, or blood-related health issues.

Mercury (Budh) – Intelligence, Communication, Business

Strong Mercury (Exalted in Virgo, Own Sign in Gemini/Virgo):

✓ Sharp intellect, excellent communication skills.

✓ Success in business, writing, teaching, and finance.

✓ Logical thinking and adaptability in life.

Weak Mercury (Debilitated in Pisces, Afflicted by Malefics):

✗ Confusion, poor decision-making, speech problems.

✗ Struggles in academics, misunderstandings in communication.

✗ Business and financial losses due to poor judgment.

Jupiter (Guru) – Wisdom, Luck, Spirituality

Strong Jupiter (Exalted in Cancer, Own Sign in Sagittarius/Pisces):

✓ Good luck, wisdom, and strong ethical values.

✓ Success in education, teaching, law, and religious fields.

✓ Happiness in family life and financial prosperity.

Weak Jupiter (Debilitated in Capricorn, Afflicted by Malefics):

✗ Lack of guidance, struggles in education and career.

✗ Financial instability and problems in marriage.

✗ Loss of faith, dishonesty, and poor decision-making.

♀ Venus (Shukra) – Love, Beauty, Luxury

Strong Venus (Exalted in Pisces, Own Sign in Taurus/Libra):

✓ Attractive personality, charm, and artistic talent.

✓ Success in love life, marriage, and creative professions.

✓ Financial stability, luxurious lifestyle, and material comfort.

Weak Venus (Debilitated in Virgo, Afflicted by Malefics):

✗ Problems in relationships and marital life.

✗ Financial losses, lack of comfort, and struggles in creative careers.

✗ Unhappiness in love and lack of emotional satisfaction.

⧗ Saturn (Shani) – Discipline, Karma, Hard Work

Strong Saturn (Exalted in Libra, Own Sign in Capricorn/Aquarius):

✓ Hardworking, disciplined, responsible.

✓ Success in long-term goals, stability, and wisdom.

✓ Strong endurance, patience, and spiritual progress.

Weak Saturn (Debilitated in Aries, Afflicted by Malefics):

✗ Delays in career, struggles in early life, financial hardships.

✗ Karma-related challenges and obstacles in major life events.

✗ Health issues related to bones, joints, and chronic diseases.

⊚ Rahu (North Node) – Desires, Materialism, Fame

Strong Rahu (Well-Placed in Taurus/Gemini, Favorable Houses):

✓ Sudden success, wealth, and recognition.

✓ Strong intuition, innovative thinking, and foreign connections.

✓ Influence in politics, technology, and social media.

Weak Rahu (Afflicted or Unfavorably Placed):

✗ Illusions, addictions, greed, and deception.

✗ Mental instability, fear, and confusion.

✗ Problems related to scandals, enemies, and hidden fears.

● Ketu (South Node) – Detachment, Spirituality, Past Karma

Strong Ketu (Well-Placed in Scorpio/Sagittarius, Favorable Houses):

✓ Deep spirituality, wisdom, and psychic abilities.

✓ Success in research, meditation, and hidden knowledge.

✓ Minimal attachment to materialistic desires.

Weak Ketu (Afflicted or Unfavorably Placed):

✗ Confusion, detachment from reality, and lack of motivation.

✗ Health issues related to digestion, anxiety, or mysterious diseases.

✗ Struggles in relationships due to detachment and lack of emotional bonding.

2. How Planetary Placements Affect Different Areas of Life

Planet	Career & Wealth	Love & Relationships	Health & Well-being
Sun	Government, leadership, politics	Authority in relationships	Heart, bones, immunity
Moon	Public relations, counseling, psychology	Emotional bonding, caring nature	Mental health, digestive system
Mars	Military, engineering, sports	Passionate relationships, aggression	Blood pressure, injuries
Mercury	Business, writing, communication	Logical approach, adaptability	Nervous system, speech issues
Jupiter	Teaching, law, finance, spirituality	Stability in marriage, wisdom	Liver, obesity, diabetes
Venus	Fashion, arts, entertainment, luxury business	Love, marriage, sensual pleasure	Skin, reproductive system
Saturn	Administration, law, labor, agriculture	Delayed marriage, stability	Bones, joints, chronic illness
Rahu	Politics, media, technology, sudden wealth	Unexpected relationships, obsessions	Psychological issues, addictions
Ketu	Research, spirituality, astrology, isolation	Detachment, karmic relationships	Mysterious diseases, spiritual healing

✥ Conclusion

✥ **Planetary placements** significantly impact different areas of life, influencing personality, career, relationships, and health.

✥ A **well-placed planet** brings success, while a **weak or afflicted planet** can create struggles.

✥ **Remedies** like mantra chanting, gemstone therapy, and spiritual practices can help balance planetary effects.

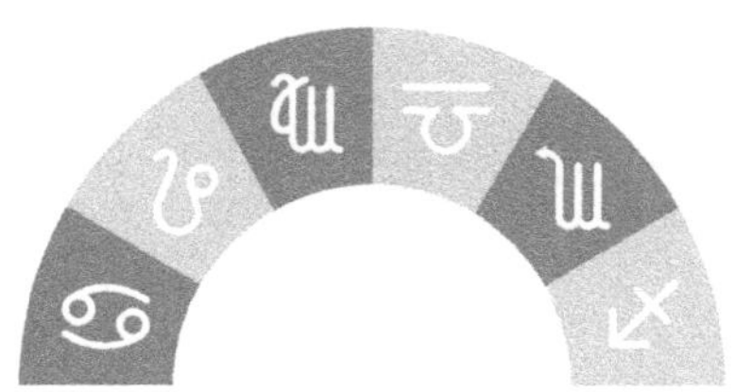

CHAPTER 4

Understanding Planetary Aspects and Conjunctions

In **Vedic astrology**, planets do not act alone—they interact with each other through **aspects (Drishti)** and **conjunctions (Yuti)**. These interactions modify their effects, influencing different areas of life, such as career, relationships, health, and wealth.

4 A) How Planets Influence Each Other

Planets influence each other in three main ways:

✓ **Through Aspects (Drishti)** – When one planet "looks" at another from a distance.

✓ **Through Conjunctions (Yuti)** – When two or more planets are in the same house.

✓ **Through Exchange (Parivartan Yoga)** – When two planets swap places, strengthening their effects.

A. Influence Through Planetary Aspects (Drishti)

In **Vedic astrology**, planets cast aspects (Drishti), influencing other planets and houses.

Each planet has a specific set of aspects:

Planet	Aspects On Houses	Influence
Sun ☼	7th house	Authority, power struggles, self-expression
Moon ☽	7th house	Emotional connection, mental influence
Mars ♂	4th, 7th, 8th houses	Aggression, energy, conflicts
Mercury ☿	7th house	Intelligence, communication, business
Jupiter ♃	5th, 7th, 9th houses	Wisdom, growth, expansion
Venus ♀	7th house	Love, creativity, romance
Saturn ♄	3rd, 7th, 10th houses	Hard work, delays, discipline
Rahu ☊	5th, 7th, 9th houses	Desires, obsession, illusion
Ketu ☋	5th, 7th, 9th houses	Detachment, spirituality, hidden knowledge

Example:

- If **Jupiter is in the 1st house**, it aspects the **5th, 7th, and 9th houses**, bringing wisdom, knowledge, and good fortune.

- If **Mars is in the 10th house**, it aspects the **4th, 7th, and 8th houses**, increasing ambition but possibly causing aggression in relationships.

◈ **Strong planets positively influence the houses they aspect** (e.g., Jupiter improves wisdom).

◈ **Malefic planets (like Saturn, Rahu, and Mars) bring challenges** but also teach important life lessons.

B. Influence Through Planetary Conjunctions (Yuti)

A **conjunction** occurs when two or more planets are in the **same house**. Their energies merge, creating unique results depending on:

- The **nature of the planets** (friendly or enemy).

- The **house they are placed in**.

- Whether the planets are **benefic (positive) or malefic (challenging)**.

Example of Conjunctions:

Conjunction	Effects
Sun + Mercury (Budh Aditya Yoga)	Sharp intellect, leadership, good communication skills.
Moon + Jupiter (Gaja Kesari Yoga)	Wisdom, emotional stability, prosperity.
Venus + Mars	Passion, strong desires, artistic talent.
Saturn + Moon (Vish Yoga)	Emotional struggles, mental stress, delays in success.
Rahu + Sun (Grahan Yoga)	Ego struggles, fame, conflicts with authority.
Ketu + Mercury	Philosophical thinking, interest in spirituality, difficulties in communication.

Example:

- **Jupiter + Venus in the 9th house** → Great for wisdom, spirituality, and luxury.

- **Mars + Saturn in the 10th house** → Creates workaholic tendencies but also career struggles.

◆ **Benefic conjunctions** bring success, wisdom, and prosperity.

◆ **Malefic conjunctions** create delays, obstacles, or struggles.

C. Influence Through Exchange (Parivartan Yoga)

Exchange (Parivartan Yoga) happens when two planets **swap houses** they are placed in. This creates a strong connection and amplifies their effects.

Example:

- **Venus in Mercury's sign (Gemini) and Mercury in Venus's sign (Taurus)** → Strong intelligence and business success.

- **Saturn in Moon's sign (Cancer) and Moon in Saturn's sign (Capricorn)** → Emotional struggles and practical mindset.

◈ **A benefic exchange strengthens both planets and gives good results.**

◈ **A malefic exchange can cause instability and difficulties.**

2. How to Interpret Planetary Influences in a Birth Chart

☑ **Step 1: Identify Planetary Placement**

- Find the **house and sign** of each planet.

- Check if the planet is **exalted (strong) or debilitated (weak)**.

☑ **Step 2: Analyse Aspects (Drishti)**

- See which houses and planets are receiving aspects.

- Determine if the aspects are **benefic (Jupiter, Venus) or malefic (Saturn, Rahu, Mars)**.

☑ **Step 3: Check for Conjunctions (Yuti)**

- Note if planets are together in the same house.

- Observe if they are **friendly or enemies**.

☑ **Step 4: Look for Exchange (Parivartan Yoga)**

- If two planets have exchanged houses, it strengthens their influence.

☑ **Step 5: Final Interpretation**

- Benefic planets bring **support, success, and positivity**.

- Malefic planets **create challenges but also push for growth and transformation**.

Example Interpretation:

- **Jupiter in the 7th house aspecting the 1st house** → A wise and supportive spouse.

- **Mars + Rahu in the 10th house** → Aggression in career, sudden rise or downfall.

✻ Conclusion

✓ **Planets influence each other through Aspects, Conjunctions, and Exchanges.**

✓ **Benefic planets (Jupiter, Venus) bring success, while malefic planets (Saturn, Mars) create challenges.**

✓ **A strong Jupiter or Venus aspect brings prosperity, while Saturn or Rahu aspects can cause delays and struggles.**

4 B) Benefic vs. Malefic Planets in Vedic Astrology

In **Vedic astrology**, planets are classified as **benefic (positive)** or **malefic (challenging)** based on their natural characteristics and how they influence human life. Benefic planets bring **growth, happiness, and fortune**, while malefic planets create **challenges, delays, and struggles** that encourage learning and growth. However, whether a planet behaves as a benefic or malefic also depends on **its placement, strength, and role in the individual's birth chart.**

1. Natural Benefic vs. Malefic Planets

✔ Natural Benefic Planets (Shubha Grahas) – Positive Influences

These planets are inherently **auspicious and supportive**, bringing **happiness, growth, and harmony** when well-placed.

Planet	Nature	Key Influences
Jupiter (Guru) 🪬	**Greatest Benefit**	Wisdom, prosperity, luck, higher knowledge
Venus (Shukra) ♀	Benefic	Love, beauty, luxury, relationships, wealth

Planet	Nature	Key Influences	
Mercury (Budh) 🌞	Benefic (when not afflicted)	Intelligence, communication, business success	
Moon (Chandra) 🌙	Benefic (when strong)	Emotional stability, nurturing energy, intuition	

Example:

- **Jupiter in the 1ˢᵗ house** (Ascendant) makes a person wise, lucky, and respected.

- **Venus in the 4ᵗʰ house** brings comfort, happiness, and a luxurious home life.

✗ Natural Malefic Planets (Paap Grahas) – Challenging Influences

These planets **bring struggles, hardships, and karmic lessons** that shape a person's character. However, when well-placed, they provide **discipline, determination, and resilience**.

Planet	Nature	Key Influences	
Saturn (Shani) ⏳	**Greatest Malefic**	Delays, discipline, karma, responsibility	
Mars (Mangal) 🔥	Malefic	Aggression, energy, war, courage	
Rahu (North Node) 🌀	Malefic	Obsession, illusion, ambition, sudden success or downfall	
Ketu (South Node) ●	Malefic	Detachment, spirituality, loss, enlightenment	
Sun (Surya) ☼	Mild Malefic	Ego, power, pride, authority	

Example:

- **Saturn in the 10ᵗʰ house** can delay career success but rewards hard work in the long run.

- **Rahu in the 7ᵗʰ house** may cause unconventional relationships or foreign partners.

2. Functional Benefic and Malefic Planets

While planets have a **natural benefic or malefic nature**, their role changes based on a person's **ascendant (Lagna)**. In every birth chart, some planets become **functional benefics** (giving good results) and **functional malefic** (causing obstacles).

A. How Functional Benefics and Malefics Are Determined

Planets that rule **good houses (Trikona and Kendra houses: 1st, 5th, 9th, 4th, 7th, and 10th)** tend to act as **benefics**.

Planets ruling **challenging houses (6th, 8th, and 12th)** act as **malefic**.

House	Effect
1st House (Lagna)	Self, health, personality
5th House (Trikona)	Intelligence, creativity, children, good karma
9th House (Trikona)	Luck, fortune, spirituality
4th House (Kendra)	Home, comfort, mother
7th House (Kendra)	Marriage, partnerships
10th House (Kendra)	Career, social status
6th House (Dushtana)	Enemies, debts, diseases (Malefic)
8th House (Dushtana)	Sudden changes, secrets, transformation (Malefic)
12th House (Dushtana)	Losses, isolation, spirituality (Malefic)

B. Benefic and Malefic Planets for Each Ascendant

Each ascendant (Lagna) has different benefic and malefic planets based on house rulership.

Example of Functional Benefic and Malefic Planets:

Ascendant	Functional Benefic Planets	Functional Malefic Planets
Aries ♈	Sun, Jupiter, Mars	Mercury, Saturn
Taurus ♉	Saturn, Mercury	Jupiter, Mars
Gemini ♊	Venus, Saturn	Mars, Jupiter

Ascendant	Functional Benefic Planets	Functional Malefic Planets
Cancer ♋	Moon, Mars	Mercury, Saturn
Leo ♌	Sun, Mars, Jupiter	Mercury, Venus
Virgo ♍	Mercury, Venus	Mars, Moon
Libra ♎	Venus, Saturn	Sun, Jupiter
Scorpio ♏	Jupiter, Sun	Mercury, Venus
Sagittarius ♐	Jupiter, Mars	Venus, Mercury
Capricorn ♑	Venus, Mercury	Jupiter, Moon
Aquarius ♒	Venus, Saturn	Sun, Mars
Pisces ♓	Jupiter, Moon	Saturn, Venus

Example:

- **For Aries Ascendant:**

  - **Jupiter (ruler of the 9th house) is a benefic.**

  - **Saturn (ruler of the 10th & 11th house) is a malefic, causing delays in career.**

- **For Libra Ascendant:**

  - **Venus (ruler of 1st house) is a benefit, supporting success.**

  - **Sun (ruler of the 11th house) is a malefic, creating ego struggles.**

3. How to Determine the Effects of Benefic and Malefic Planets in a Birth Chart

To analyze how a planet will behave in a chart, follow these steps:

✅ Step 1: Identify Natural Benefic and Malefic Planets

- Look at **Jupiter, Venus, Mercury, and Moon** for positive influences.

- Check **Saturn, Mars, Rahu, Ketu, and Sun** for challenging influences.

☑ Step 2: Check Functional Benefic and Malefic Planets for the Ascendant

- Find which planets rule the **Trikona (5th, 9th) and Kendra (1st, 4th, 7th, 10th) houses.**

- Identify which planets rule **6th, 8th, and 12th houses**—these act as malefics.

☑ Step 3: Analyse the Placement of the Planets

- **Well-placed benefics** (exalted, own sign, or good houses) bring prosperity.

- **Afflicted benefics** (debilitated, combusted, or in bad houses) lose power.

- **Well-placed malefic** (exalted, own sign) provide strength and discipline.

- **Afflicted malefic** (weak or in bad houses) creates struggles.

Example Analysis:

- **Jupiter in the 9th house (its own sign, Sagittarius) → Brings great luck and prosperity.**

- **Saturn in the 8th house → Creates struggles, delays, and karmic lessons.**

✨ Conclusion

✓ **Benefic planets bring support, growth, and harmony, while malefic planets bring challenges and karmic lessons.**

✓ **Each ascendant has different functional benefic and malefic planets.**

✓ **A well-placed benefic planet brings prosperity, while an afflicted benefic loses power.**

✓ **A strong malefic can provide discipline and endurance, while a weak malefic can create unnecessary obstacles.**

4 C) What Are Yogas in Vedic Astrology?

In Vedic astrology, *Yoga* refers to special planetary combinations or alignments that influence a person's life in significant ways. The term "Yoga" means *union* or *combination*, and in astrology, it signifies the relationship between planets, houses, and signs that create specific outcomes—whether positive (Raj Yoga, Dhan Yoga) or challenging (Daridra Yoga, Grahan Yoga).

These Yogas can indicate **wealth, power, intelligence, fame, struggles, or obstacles** depending on their nature and strength in a birth chart (*kundli*). They play a crucial role in shaping a person's destiny, but their effects can vary based on planetary strength, aspects, and other influences in the chart.

How Are Yogas Formed?

Yogas are formed in different ways, including:

1. **Placement of Planets** – When certain planets occupy specific houses or signs.

2. **Mutual Relationship** – When planets are in conjunction, aspect each other, or are in exchange (*parivartan yoga*).

3. **House Combinations** – When certain houses (like the 1st, 5th, 9th for success or 2nd, 11th for wealth) interact positively.

4. **Strength of Planets** – Yogas give better results when involved planets are strong (in exaltation, own sign, or in friendly houses).

Types of Yogas in Vedic Astrology

Yogas can be broadly classified into **beneficial (Shubha Yogas)** and **challenging (Ashubha Yogas)**.

1. Beneficial Yogas (Shubha Yogas)

These yogas bring success, prosperity, and growth:

- **Raj Yoga** – Brings power, leadership, and success.

- **Dhan Yoga** – Gives financial prosperity.

- **Gajakesari Yoga** – Bestows intelligence, wisdom, and wealth.

- **Lakshmi Yoga** – Provides luxury and financial abundance.

- **Panch Mahapurusha Yoga** – Creates extraordinary individuals with great skills and influence.

2. Challenging Yogas (Ashubha Yogas)

These can bring struggles but can be overcome with remedies:

- **Daridra Yoga** – Causes financial difficulties.

- **Grahan Yoga** – Created by Rahu/Ketu with the Sun or Moon, leading to emotional and mental struggles.

- **Kemadruma Yoga** – Bring loneliness and financial instability if the Moon is weak.

- **Shakata Yoga** – Brings ups and downs in life.

Raj Yoga in Vedic Astrology: The Yoga of Power and Success

Raj Yoga (राज योग) is one of the most powerful and auspicious planetary combinations in Vedic astrology. It bestows **success, authority, wealth, fame, and leadership** to the natives. The word *Raj* means "king," and *Yoga* means "union" or "combination," so Raj Yoga signifies the "Yoga of Kings," indicating royal status, high achievements, and prosperity.

How Is Raj Yoga Formed?

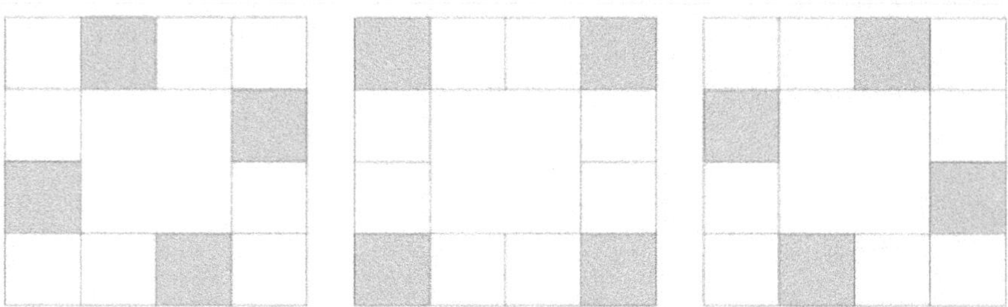

Raj Yoga is formed when **beneficial relationships occur between the Kendra (1st, 4th, 7th, 10th) and Trikona (1st, 5th, 9th) houses**. These houses are considered powerful in a birth chart:

- **Kendra Houses (1st, 4th, 7th, 10th)** – Represent strength, stability, and action.

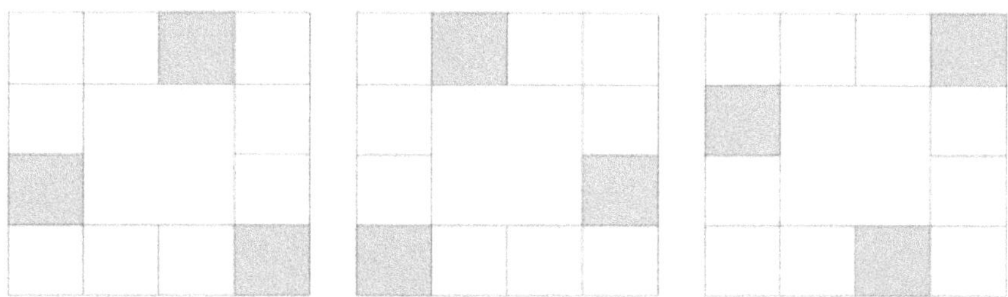

- **Trikona Houses (1ˢᵗ, 5ᵗʰ, 9ᵗʰ)** – Represent luck, wisdom, and divine blessings.

A Raj Yoga occurs when:

☑ **Lords of Kendra and Trikona houses combine exchange signs, or aspect each other.**

☑ **Strong and benefic planets (like Jupiter, Venus, and Moon) form a connection with these houses.**

☑ **A planet is exalted or in its sign while forming this Yoga.**

Example: If the **9ᵗʰ house lord (fortune) is in the 10ᵗʰ house (career) and the 10ᵗʰ house lord is in the 9ᵗʰ house**, it forms a powerful Raj Yoga, bringing career success and recognition.

Types of Raj Yoga

There are many types of Raj Yogas based on planetary combinations. Some of the most powerful include:

1. Kendra-Trikona Raj Yoga

- Formed when **Kendra and Trikona lords combine** (like 9ᵗʰ and 10ᵗʰ house lords together).

- Brings success, prosperity, and power.

- Strongest when the planets involved are exalted or in their sign.

2. Raja Lakshmana Yoga

- When **the lord of the ascendant (Lagna) is in the 10ᵗʰ house (Karma Bhava)**.

- The person becomes a leader, CEO, or authority figure.

3. Dharma-Karma Adhipati Yoga

- When the **9th lord (dharma)** and **10th lord (karma) exchange signs** or form a conjunction.

- Bring great name, fame, and career success.

4. Vipreet Raj Yoga (*Success after Struggle*)

- Formed when lords of the **6th, 8th, or 12th houses** are placed in those houses themselves.

- It initially brings struggles, but later leads to great success after hardships.

- Example: If the 8th lord is in the 8th house (in its sign), the person overcomes challenges and rises to power.

5. Neecha Bhanga Raj Yoga (*Cancellation of Debilitation*)

- If a debilitated planet (weak) is supported by certain conditions (like exalted planets in the same sign), it cancels the weakness and gives Raj Yoga effects.

- Example: If a debilitated Saturn in Aries is affected by a strong Mars, its negative effects are canceled, leading to success.

Effects of Raj Yoga on a Birth Chart

The impact of Raj Yoga depends on **planetary strength, Dasha periods, and transits**. If strongly present, it gives:

✔ **Wealth & prosperity** – Financial stability and luxury.

✔ **Authority & power** – Leadership positions, government jobs, or high status.

✔ **Fame & Recognition** – The person gains respect and honor in society.

✔ **career success** – A rise in profession or entrepreneurship.

Examples of Raj Yoga in Famous Personalities' Charts

◆ **Narendra Modi (Indian Prime Minister)** – Has a powerful Raj Yoga due to a strong 10th house and Jupiter's influence.

◆ **Amitabh Bachchan (Actor)** – Raj Yoga is formed in his chart due to strong Jupiter and Saturn positions.

◆ **Bill Gates (Entrepreneur)** – Raj Yoga helped him achieve immense wealth and success.

How to Strengthen Raj Yoga?

Even if Raj Yoga is present in a birth chart, it may not activate unless the right **dasha (planetary period)** is running. To enhance its effects:

☑ **Strengthen weak planets** with **gemstones** (like Yellow Sapphire for Jupiter).

☑ **Chant mantras** like **"Om Namo Bhagavate Vasudevaya"** for Jupiter or "Om Sham Shanicharaya Namah" for Saturn.

Dhan Yoga in Vedic Astrology: The Yoga of Wealth and Prosperity

Dhan Yoga (धन योग) is one of the most important planetary combinations in Vedic astrology that brings **wealth, financial stability, and prosperity**. The word *Dhan* means "money" or "wealth," and *Yoga* refers to a special planetary alignment. People with strong Dhan Yoga in their birth chart (*kundli*) often experience financial success, luxury, and material abundance.

How Is Dhan Yoga Formed?

Dhan Yoga occurs when planets connected to **wealth-giving houses (2nd, 11th, 5th, 9th)** are well-placed, strong, and positively influence each other.

Key Houses Responsible for Wealth in a Birth Chart

💰 **2ⁿᵈ House (Dhana Bhava)** – Represents **accumulated wealth, savings, and family assets.**

💰 **11ᵗʰ House (Labha Bhava)** – Indicates **income, financial gains, and profits.**

💰 **5ᵗʰ House (Purva Punya Bhava)** – Shows **intelligence, luck, and speculative gains (like stock market, lottery, or investments).**

💰 **9ᵗʰ House (Bhagya Bhava)** – Represents **fortune, destiny, and financial blessings from past karma.**

💰 **10ᵗʰ House (Karma Bhava)** – Connected to **career and professional earnings.**

Dhan Yoga is formed when:

✅ The **2ⁿᵈ and 11ᵗʰ house lords** are connected (by conjunction, exchange, or aspect).

✅ The **9ᵗʰ and 5ᵗʰ house lords** form a relation with **2ⁿᵈ or 11ᵗʰ house.**

✅ A **strong Jupiter, Venus, Mercury, or Moon** is placed in a wealth-giving house.

✅ A benefic planet is **exalted, in its sign, or a friendly sign** in these houses.

Example: If the **2ⁿᵈ lord is in the 11ᵗʰ house** and the **11ᵗʰ lord is in the 2ⁿᵈ house**, this creates a strong Dhan Yoga, ensuring financial success.

Types of Dhan Yoga

1. Classical Dhan Yoga (2ⁿᵈ & 11ᵗʰ House Connection)

- If **the 2ⁿᵈ lord is in the 11ᵗʰ house** or vice versa, strong financial gains are assured.

- Example: **Taurus Ascendant – If Mercury (2ⁿᵈ lord) is placed in the 11ᵗʰ house (Pisces),** this creates a powerful wealth yoga.

2. Lakshmi Yoga *(Wealth and Luxury)*

- Formed when **the 9th lord (luck) is strong and in its own/exalted sign, and the ascendant is also strong**.

- Brings immense financial blessings, luxury, and prosperity.

- Example: If **Jupiter (9th lord) is in the 5th house, well-placed and strong**, Lakshmi Yoga is formed.

3. Chandra-Mangal Dhan Yoga *(Business and Wealth Generation)*

- Occurs when the **Moon and Mars are together in any house**.

- Gives a strong business mindset and financial gains from entrepreneurship.

- Example: If the **Moon and Mars are in the 2nd house**, it creates massive earning potential.

4. Gajakesari Yoga *(Wealth through Intelligence and Wisdom)*

- Formed when **Jupiter is in a Kendra (1st, 4th, 7th, 10th) from the Moon**.

- Brings financial success, wisdom, and leadership in wealth management.

- Example: If **Jupiter is in the 4th house and Moon is in the 1st house**, Gajakesari Yoga forms.

5. Parivartan Dhan Yoga *(Exchange Yoga for Wealth)*

- If the **2nd house lord and 11th house lord exchange signs**, wealth is multiplied.

- Example: In **Aries Ascendant, if Venus (2nd lord) is in Aquarius and Saturn (11th lord) is in Taurus**, this forms a wealth-giving Parivartan Yoga.

Effects of Dhan Yoga on a Birth Chart

The impact of Dhan Yoga depends on **planetary strength, Dasha periods, and transits**. If strongly present, it gives:

✔ **Wealth and financial stability** – Strong savings, multiple income sources, and material comforts.

✔ **Success in business and investments** – Luck in trading, stock markets, and entrepreneurship.

✔ **Luxury and prosperity** – Enjoyment of expensive items, real estate, and a high standard of living.

✔ **Generational wealth** – Ability to build and pass on assets to future generations.

Famous People with Dhan Yoga

◆ **Mukesh Ambani (Billionaire, Business Tycoon)** – Strong Dhan Yoga due to the 2nd and 11th house connection.

◆ **Bill Gates (Founder of Microsoft)** – Wealth-giving planetary combinations with Jupiter's strong influence.

◆ **Warren Buffett (Investor)** – Dhan Yoga through the 2nd house and Mercury's strength in finance-related houses.

How to Strengthen Dhan Yoga?

Even if Dhan Yoga is present in a birth chart, its effects may not manifest unless the right **dasha (planetary period)** is running. To enhance its effects:

☑ **Strengthen weak planets** with **gemstones** (like Yellow Sapphire for Jupiter, Emerald for Mercury).

☑ **Chant wealth mantras** like **"Om Shreem Mahalakshmiye Namah"** or "Om Brihaspataye Namah" for Jupiter.

☑ **Donate to charities** – Giving back strengthens financial karma.

☑ **Invest wisely** – Utilize financial knowledge and make smart investment decisions.

☑ **Perform remedies** – Such as fasting on **Fridays (for Venus) or Thursdays (for Jupiter)** to attract prosperity.

✤ **Conclusion**

Dhan Yoga is a powerful indicator of wealth and financial success in a birth chart. However, **hard work, karma, and smart financial planning** also play a crucial role in achieving prosperity. Even if a person has strong Dhan Yoga, **their financial potential is best realized through wise investments and efforts**.

Gajakesari Yoga in Vedic Astrology: The Yoga of Intelligence, Wealth, and Fame

Gajakesari Yoga (*गजकेसरी योग*) is one of the most powerful and auspicious yogas in Vedic astrology. It brings **wisdom, wealth, intelligence, success, and respect** to the natives.

The name *Gajakesari* comes from two Sanskrit words:

- **Gaja (गज)** – Meaning *elephant*, symbolizing **strength and intelligence**.

- **Kesari (केसरी)** – Meaning *lion*, symbolizing **courage and leadership**.

Together, this yoga represents a person who possesses the **strength of an elephant and the royal presence of a lion**, making them **wise, influential, and successful** in life.

How Is Gajakesari Yoga Formed?

This yoga is formed when **Jupiter (Guru) is in a Kendra (1ˢᵗ, 4ᵗʰ, 7ᵗʰ, or 10ᵗʰ house) from the Moon (Chandra)** in a birth chart (*Kundli*).

Key Conditions for a Strong Gajakesari Yoga:

☑ **Jupiter should be in 1ˢᵗ, 4ᵗʰ, 7ᵗʰ, or 10ᵗʰ house from the Moon.**

☑ **Jupiter should be strong** (exalted, in its sign, or friendly sign).

☑ **Moon should also be well-placed** (not debilitated or afflicted by malefic planets like Rahu, Ketu, or Saturn).

☑ **No malefic aspects from Saturn, Rahu, or Ketu on Jupiter or Moon.**

Example: If the **Moon is in Aries (1ˢᵗ house) and Jupiter is in Cancer (4ᵗʰ house)**, this forms a **powerful Gajakesari Yoga** because Cancer is Jupiter's exaltation sign, making the yoga stronger.

Effects of Gajakesari Yoga

If this yoga is strong in a birth chart, it gives:

✔ **Wealth and Prosperity** – The person enjoys financial stability and abundance.

✔ **Wisdom and Intelligence** – They have deep knowledge, sharp intellect, and a philosophical mindset.

✔ **Fame and Recognition** – They gain respect in society and may become well-known personalities.

✔ **Leadership and Power** – Many political leaders, business tycoons, and spiritual gurus have this yoga.

✔ **Good Fortune and Luck** – The person receives blessings, good opportunities, and success in life.

✔ **Strong Communication Skills** – They can be excellent teachers, speakers, or writers.

Famous Personalities with Gajakesari Yoga

◈ **Swami Vivekananda** – His intelligence, wisdom, and leadership qualities were enhanced by Gajakesari Yoga.

◈ **Sachin Tendulkar** – His fame and success in cricket were supported by this yoga.

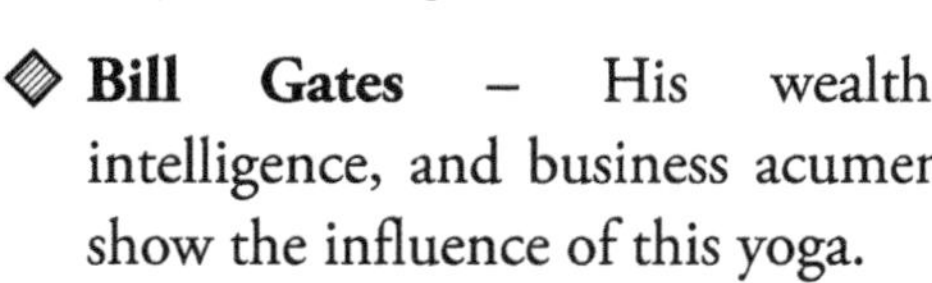

◈ **Barack Obama** – His strong communication skills and leadership qualities are linked to Gajakesari Yoga.

◈ **Bill Gates** – His wealth, intelligence, and business acumen show the influence of this yoga.

Weak vs. Strong Gajakesari Yoga

Even if Gajakesari Yoga is present in a chart, its strength depends on the condition of Jupiter and the Moon:

A Strong Gajakesari Yoga (Highly Beneficial)

☑ Jupiter is **exalted (Cancer)** or in its sign (**Sagittarius, Pisces**).

☑ Moon is **well-placed, strong, and unafflicted.**

☑ The yoga occurs in **important houses** (1st, 5th, 9th, or 10th house).

☑ The person experiences **immense success, intelligence, and prosperity.**

A Weak Gajakesari Yoga (Less Effective)

✗ Jupiter is **debilitated (Capricorn)** or afflicted by malefic planets like **Saturn, Rahu, or Ketu.**

✗ Moon is **weak (debilitated in Scorpio) or placed in the 6th, 8th, or 12th house.**

✗ The person may still have **intelligence and wisdom** but might struggle to achieve success easily.

How to Strengthen Gajakesari Yoga?

If Gajakesari Yoga is weak in a chart, its effects can be enhanced through **astrological remedies:**

☑ **Worship Lord Vishnu and Goddess Saraswati** for wisdom and intelligence.

☑ **Chant "Om Brihaspataye Namah" (for Jupiter) and "Om Chandraya Namah" (for Moon) daily.**

☑ **Wear a Yellow Sapphire (for Jupiter) or Pearl (for Moon)** if recommended by an astrologer.

☑ **Observe fasts on Thursdays (for Jupiter) and Mondays (for Moon).**

☑ **Donate yellow items (turmeric, bananas) on Thursdays** to strengthen Jupiter.

✿ Conclusion

Gajakesari Yoga is a highly auspicious combination in Vedic astrology, bringing **intelligence, fame, success, and financial growth**. However, its power depends on **planetary strength, house placement, and dasha periods**. While this yoga can give great fortune, **hard work, good karma, and wise decisions** are also necessary for long-term success.

Lakshmi Yoga in Vedic Astrology: The Yoga of Wealth, Prosperity, and Fortune

Lakshmi Yoga (*लक्ष्मी योग*) is one of the most powerful **Dhan Yogas** in Vedic astrology, bringing **immense wealth, luxury, prosperity, and good fortune** to a person. Named after **Goddess Lakshmi**, the deity of wealth and abundance, this yoga blesses an individual with **financial success, material comforts, and a high social status**.

How Is Lakshmi Yoga Formed?

Lakshmi Yoga is formed when the following conditions are met:

- ☑ The 9th house lord (Bhagya Bhava – House of Fortune) is strong and well-placed.

- ☑ The lord of the 9th house is in its sign, exalted, or in a friendly sign.

- ☑ The ascendant (Lagna) and its lord should also be strong and unafflicted.

- ☑ A benefic planet (Jupiter, Venus, Mercury, or Moon) should be involved.

Example: If a person has a **Leo Ascendant and Jupiter (9th house lord) is exalted in Cancer (in the 12th house)**, it creates a strong Lakshmi Yoga, ensuring immense financial success.

Effects of Lakshmi Yoga

If this yoga is strong in a birth chart, it brings:

- ✔ **Massive Wealth & Prosperity** – The person accumulates huge financial gains.

- ✔ **Luxurious Lifestyle** – Enjoys expensive possessions, real estate, and comforts.

- ✔ **Good Fortune & Luck** – Success comes easily, and opportunities flow naturally.

✔ **Power & Respect** – The person gains a high social status and influence.

✔ **Success in Business & Investments** – They are skilled in managing money and growing wealth.

✔ **Spiritual Growth** – Along with material wealth, they may also develop strong spiritual inclinations.

Famous Personalities with Lakshmi Yoga

◈ **Mukesh Ambani** – One of the richest people in the world, has strong wealth yogas in his chart.

◈ **Bill Gates** – His intelligence and financial success are influenced by strong Dhan Yogas, possibly including Lakshmi Yoga.

◈ **Warren Buffett** – His ability to generate and sustain wealth aligns with this yoga.

Strengthening Lakshmi Yoga

If Lakshmi Yoga is weak or not fully activated in a birth chart, it can be strengthened through:

☑ **Worshipping Goddess Lakshmi** – Chanting the **Lakshmi Mantra**:

"Om Shreem Mahalakshmiye Namah" daily for prosperity.

☑ **Wearing a Yellow Sapphire (Pukhraj)** – If Jupiter is the 9th house lord in the chart.

☑ **Observing fasts on Thursdays** – To strengthen Jupiter (if involved).

☑ **Performing charity and donations** – Giving to the needy attracts good karma and financial blessings.

☑ **Keeping the house clean and placing a Shri Yantra** – To invite positive energy and abundance.

✿ Conclusion

Lakshmi Yoga is a rare and powerful wealth yoga that blesses individuals with **immense prosperity, luck, and a high standard of living**. However, for it to be fully effective, **hard work, karma, and wise financial management** are equally important.

Panch Mahapurusha Yoga in Vedic Astrology: The Yoga of Greatness and Influence

Panch Mahapurusha Yoga (पंच महापुरुष योग) is one of the most powerful and auspicious yogas in Vedic astrology. It is formed by the placement of five major planets—**Mars, Mercury, Jupiter, Venus, and Saturn**—in specific strong positions.

People born with this yoga often achieve **great success, power, intelligence, and influence**, becoming extraordinary individuals (*Mahapurush* means "great person"). Many famous leaders, scholars, and successful personalities have one or more of these yogas in their birth charts.

How Is Panch Mahapurusha Yoga Formed?

Panch Mahapurusha Yoga occurs when any of the following planets—**Mars, Mercury, Jupiter, Venus, or Saturn**—is:

✅ **In its sign or exalted** (Mars in Aries/Scorpio, Mercury in Gemini/Virgo, Jupiter in Sagittarius/Pisces, Venus in Taurus/Libra, Saturn in Capricorn/Aquarius).

✅ **Placed in a Kendra house** (1st, 4th, 7th, or 10th house) from the Ascendant (*Lagna*).

Each planet forms a unique Mahapurusha Yoga, influencing different aspects of life.

Types of Panch Mahapurusha Yoga & Their Effects

1. Ruchaka Yoga (Mars) – The Warrior's Strength 💪 🔥

- Formed when **Mars is in a Kendra (1st, 4th, 7th, or 10th house) in Aries, Scorpio, or Capricorn (exalted)**.

- Brings **courage, leadership, military or sports success, and a strong physique**.

- People with this yoga are **brave, energetic, determined, and powerful leaders**.

- **Famous Personalities:** Napoleon Bonaparte, Indira Gandhi, sports champions.

2. Bhadra Yoga (Mercury) – The Genius Mind 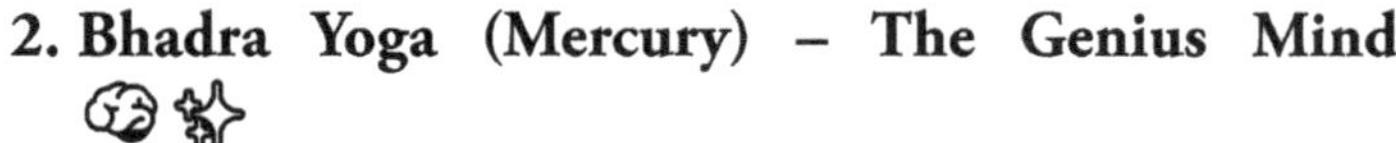

- Formed when **Mercury is in a Kendra house in Gemini or Virgo (exalted in Virgo)**.

- Gives **intelligence, sharp memory, communication skills, and business acumen**.

- People with this yoga are **great speakers, writers, businessmen, and strategists**.

- **Famous Personalities:** Bill Gates, and Mark Zuckerberg, successful entrepreneurs.

3. Hamsa Yoga (Jupiter) – The Divine Blessing 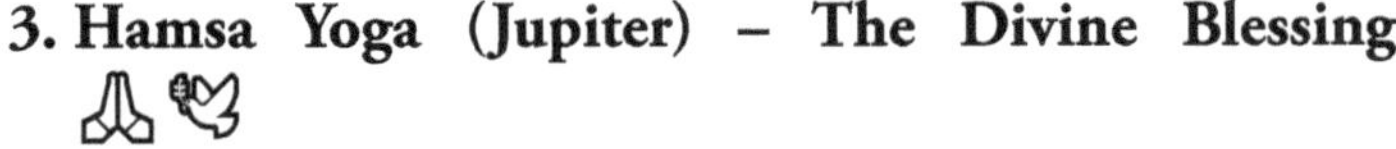

- Formed when **Jupiter is in a Kendra house in Sagittarius, Pisces, or Cancer (exalted in Cancer)**.

- Bestows **spiritual wisdom, righteousness, prosperity, and a noble character**.

- People with this yoga often become **spiritual leaders, scholars, or highly respected individuals**.

- **Famous Personalities:** Swami Vivekananda, Dalai Lama, **wise scholars** and teachers.

4. Malavya Yoga (Venus) – The Beauty and Luxury 💝 🏵

- Formed when **Venus is in a Kendra house in Taurus, Libra, or Pisces (exalted in Pisces).**

- Brings **charm, beauty, artistic talent, wealth, and luxurious comforts.**

- People with this yoga excel in **fashion, entertainment, music, and creativity.**

- **Famous Personalities:** Marilyn Monroe, famous actors, artists, and luxury business owners.

5. Shasha Yoga (Saturn) – The Kingmaker 🏛 ♆

- Formed when **Saturn is in a Kendra house in Capricorn, Aquarius, or Libra (exalted in Libra).**

- Bring **discipline, patience, leadership, and long-term success.**

- People with this yoga often **rise to power after struggles and become great leaders.**

- **Famous Personalities:** Abraham Lincoln, Nelson Mandela, successful politicians and business moguls.

Strength of Panch Mahapurusha Yoga

The effects of this yoga depend on:

☑ **Strength of the planet** – Exalted planets give the most powerful results.

☑ **House placement** – In the 1st or 10th house, it is especially strong.

☑ **Aspect and conjunctions** – If malefic planets (like Rahu or Ketu) afflict it, the yoga may weaken.

☑ **Dasha periods (Planetary cycles)** – The effects are most visible during the major period (*Mahadasha*) of the planet-forming yoga.

How to Strengthen Panch Mahapurusha Yoga?

If this yoga is weak in a chart, its effects can be enhanced through:

☑ **Chanting Planetary Mantras**:

- **Mars (Ruchaka Yoga):** "Om Angarakaya Namah" (for strength and courage).

- **Mercury (Bhadra Yoga):** "Om Budhaya Namah" (for intelligence and success).

- **Jupiter (Hamsa Yoga):** "Om Brihaspataye Namah" (for wisdom and blessings).

- **Venus (Malavya Yoga):** "Om Shukraya Namah" (for beauty and wealth).

- **Saturn (Shasha Yoga):** "Om Sham Shanicharaya Namah" (for discipline and power).

☑ **Wearing appropriate gemstones** (under expert guidance):

- **Mars:** Red Coral

- **Mercury:** Emerald

- **Jupiter:** Yellow Sapphire

- **Venus:** Diamond or White Sapphire

- **Saturn:** Blue Sapphire

☑ **Donating items related to the planet** on specific days (e.g., donating yellow items on Thursday for Jupiter).

☑ **Performing Pooja and Homas** to strengthen the beneficial influence of these planets.

✤ **Conclusion**

Panch Mahapurusha Yoga is a **rare and powerful combination** that creates highly influential and successful individuals. However, **karma, hard work, and planetary strength** also play an essential role in determining the full impact of this yoga.

Challenging Yogas (Ashubha Yogas) in Vedic Astrology

While astrology reveals many **prosperous yogas** that bring success and fortune, it also identifies **challenging yogas (Ashubha Yogas)** that create obstacles, struggles, and hardships in life. These yogas arise due to **afflicted planets, weak house placements, and negative planetary combinations**, leading to financial problems, health issues, emotional instability, and delays in success. However, remedies and personal effort can **reduce or neutralize their effects**.

1. Grahan Yoga (Eclipse Yoga) – Mental & Emotional Struggles

- ◈ **Formation:** Occurs when **Rahu or Ketu is conjunct with the Sun or Moon** in a birth chart.

- ◈ **Effects:** Causes **mental stress, confusion, emotional instability, and health issues.** The person may struggle with decision-making and face constant ups and downs.

- ◈ **Remedies:**

- ✔ Worship **Lord Shiva or Goddess Durga** to balance eclipse effects.

- ✔ Chant **"Om Namah Shivaya"** or "Om Suryaaya Namah" (for Sun) and "Om Somaya Namah" (for Moon).

- ✔ Avoid making big decisions on eclipses.

2. Kemadruma Yoga – Loneliness & Financial Instability

- ◈ **Formation:** This occurs when **there are no planets (except Rahu/Ketu) on both sides of the Moon** in a birth chart.

- ◈ **Effects:** Causes **loneliness, financial struggles, and emotional instability.** The person may lack mental peace and feel isolated.

- ◈ **Remedies:**

- ✔ Keep a **silver item** with you (strengthens the Moon).

- ✔ Chant **"Om Chandraya Namah"** and wear a Pearl (if suitable).

- ✔ Engage in **charitable activities and meditation** to balance emotions.

3. Daridra Yoga – Financial Struggles & Poverty

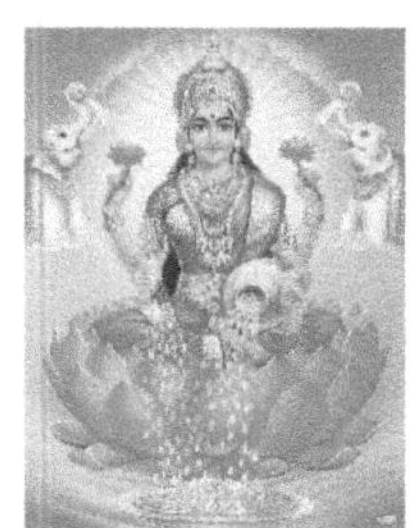

◈ **Formation:** This happens when **the 2nd (wealth) and 11th (income) house lords are weak, afflicted, or placed in dusthana houses (6th, 8th, or 12th).**

◈ **Effects:** Causes **financial instability, debt, and loss of wealth.**

◈ **Remedies:**

☑ Worship **Mahalakshmi** and chant **"Om Shreem Mahalakshmiye Namah."**

☑ Avoid unethical financial dealings and invest wisely.

☑ Strengthen wealth-related planets (Jupiter, Venus).

4. Vish Yoga – Toxicity & Struggles

◈ **Formation:** When **the Moon and Saturn are together** in a birth chart.

◈ **Effects:** Brings **negativity, depression, mental stress, and delays in success.**

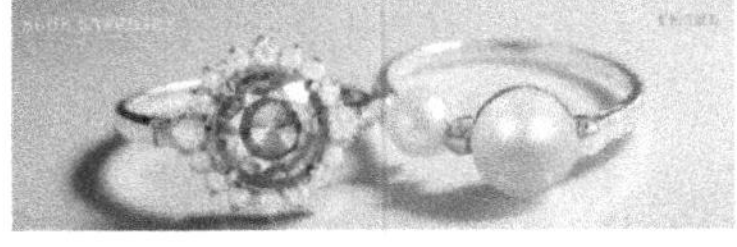

◈ **Remedies:**

☑ Worship **Lord Shiva** and chant the **Mahamrityunjaya Mantra.**

☑ Perform Rudrabhishek (Shiva Abhishek) on Mondays.

☑ Wear a **Blue Sapphire or Pearl** (if recommended).

5. Pitra Dosha – Ancestors' Karmic Debt

◈ **Formation:** When **the Sun is afflicted by Rahu/Ketu or placed in the 9th house (house of ancestors).**

◈ **Effects:** Bring **family issues, delays in career, and financial troubles** due to past-life karmic imbalances.

◈ **Remedies:**

☑ Perform **Pitra Tarpan (ancestral rituals)**, especially during **Pitru Paksha.**

☑ Donate food to **Brahmins or needy people.**

☑ Chant **"Om Pitribhyo Namah"** on Amavasya (new moon day).

6. Kaal Sarp Dosh – Struggles & Delayed Success

◈ **Formation:** When **all planets are placed between Rahu and Ketu** in a birth chart.

◈ **Effects:** Causes **delays in success, struggles, health problems, and obstacles** in life.

◈ **Remedies:**

☑ Perform **Kaal Sarp Dosh Puja** in **Trimbakeshwar (Nashik) or Ujjain.**

☑ Chant **"Om Rahave Namah"** and **"Om Ketave Namah."**

☑ Wear a **Gomed (Hessonite) or Cat's Eye (Lehsunia)** if suitable.

7. Shakata Yoga – Frequent Ups & Downs

◈ **Formation:** When **Jupiter is in the 6th, 8th, or 12th house from the Moon.**

◈ **Effects:** Brings **fluctuations in fortune, career instability, and delays in achieving goals.**

◈ **Remedies:**

☑ Worship **Lord Vishnu** and chant **Vishnu Sahasranama.**

☑ Wear a **Yellow Sapphire (if Jupiter is not weak).**

☑ Donate **yellow items (turmeric, bananas) on Thursdays.**

✨ Conclusion

Challenging Yogas in astrology can create obstacles, but **they are not absolute.** With **the right remedies, effort, and spiritual practices,** their negative effects can be minimized, and one can still lead a successful and fulfilling life.

Divisional Charts in Vedic Astrology (Varga Charts)

In **Vedic Astrology (Jyotish)**, divisional charts, also known as **Varga charts**, are derived from the main birth chart (D1 or Rashi chart) by dividing each sign into multiple sections. These charts help astrologers analyze different aspects of a person's life with greater detail and precision.

Each divisional chart focuses on a specific area of life, such as career, relationships, wealth, spiritual growth, etc. A thorough analysis of the birth chart along with the divisional charts provides a more nuanced and accurate reading.

✨ Why Are Divisional Charts Important?

1. **Micro-Level Analysis:** They provide deeper insights into specific life aspects that are not fully visible in the main birth chart.
2. **Verification of Promises:** Divisional charts confirm or modify the results indicated in the main chart.
3. **Predictive Accuracy:** They refine predictions and rectify birth times for greater accuracy.

📚 How Are Divisional Charts Formed?

Each sign (30°) is divided into different equal parts to create the various divisional charts. The degrees of the planet in the birth chart determine its position in the corresponding divisional chart.

For example:

- If a planet is at 15° in Aries (Mesha Rashi), and if we are constructing the **Navamsa chart (D9)**, we place that planet in the corresponding Navamsa sign based on its degree.

📊 Main Divisional Charts and Their Significance

1. D1 – Rashi Chart (Lagna Chart)

- **Purpose:** Represents the overall life, personality, physical body, and general trajectory.
- **Division:** 12 Signs, 30° each.

2. D2 – Hora Chart

- **Purpose:** Indicates wealth, family inheritance, and sustenance.
- **Division:** Each sign is divided into 2 parts (15° each).
- **Calculation:**
  - Odd signs: First 15° ruled by Sun, next 15° ruled by Moon.
  - Even signs: First 15° ruled by Moon, next 15° ruled by Sun.

3. D3 – Drekkana Chart

- **Purpose:** Siblings, co-borns, and courage.
- **Division:** Each sign is divided into 3 parts (10° each).
- **Rules:**
  - First Drekkana: Same sign.
  - Second Drekkana: 5th sign from the original sign.
  - Third Drekkana: 9th sign from the original sign.

4. D4 – Chaturthamsa/Chaturthamsa (Padma)

- **Purpose:** Property, assets, real estate, and fortune.
- **Division:** Each sign is divided into 4 parts (7°30' each).

5. D5 – Panchamsa Chart

- **Purpose:** Power, authority, and recognition.
- **Division:** Each sign is divided into 5 parts (6° each).

6. D6 – Shashtamsa Chart

- **Purpose:** Health, diseases, obstacles, and enemies.
- **Division:** Each sign is divided into 6 parts (5° each).

7. D7 – Saptamsa Chart

- **Purpose:** Children, progeny, creativity, and lineage.
- **Division:** Each sign is divided into 7 parts (~4°17' each).

8. D8 – Ashtamsa/Ashtamsha Chart (Kalamsa)

- **Purpose:** Longevity, obstacles, and unexpected events.
- **Division:** Each sign is divided into 8 parts (3°45' each).

9. D9 – Navamsa Chart

- **Purpose:** Marriage, relationships, spiritual growth, and Dharma.
- **Division:** Each sign is divided into 9 parts (3°20' each).
- **Importance:**
  - Confirms promises of the Rashi chart.
  - Analyzes marriage and partnerships.
  - Evaluates planetary strength through **Vargottama** (same sign in D1 and D9).

10. D10 – Dasamsa Chart (Dashamsha)

- **Purpose:** Career, profession, social status, and reputation.
- **Division:** Each sign is divided into 10 parts (3° each).
- **Importance:**
  - Provides insights into career growth, fame, and public life.
  - Analyzes Mahadasha effects on career.

11. D12 – Dwadashamsa Chart (Suryamsa)

- **Purpose:** Parents, ancestors, and karmic inheritance.
- **Division:** Each sign is divided into 12 parts (2°30' each).

12. D16 – Shodashamsa Chart (Kalamsa)

- **Purpose:** Vehicles, comforts, and luxuries.
- **Division:** Each sign is divided into 16 parts (1°52'30" each).

13. D20 – Vimsamsa Chart

- **Purpose:** Spiritual pursuits, devotion, and religious inclinations.
- **Division:** Each sign is divided into 20 parts (1°30' each).

14. D24 – Chaturvimsamsa Chart

- **Purpose:** Education, knowledge, and learning.
- **Division:** Each sign is divided into 24 parts (1°15' each).

15. D27 – Bhamsa Chart

- **Purpose:** Strength, valor, and physical capability.
- **Division:** Each sign is divided into 27 parts (1°06'40" each).

16. D30 – Trimsamsa Chart

- **Purpose:** Misfortunes, adversity, and challenges.
- **Division:** Each sign is divided into 30 parts (1° each).
- **Unique Rule:**
  - Mars, Saturn, Mercury, Jupiter, and Venus govern different parts of odd and even signs.

17. D40 – Khavedamsa Chart

- **Purpose:** Ancestral blessings and curses.
- **Division:** Each sign is divided into 40 parts (0°45' each).

18. D45 – Akshavedamsa Chart

- **Purpose:** Spiritual potential and mental inclinations.
- **Division:** Each sign is divided into 45 parts (~0°40' each).

19. D60 – Shashtiamsa Chart

- **Purpose:** Past life karma and detailed spiritual insights.
- **Division:** Each sign is divided into 60 parts (0°30' each).
- **Importance:**
  - Considered highly significant for karmic analysis.
  - Used in birth time rectification.

📊 How to Calculate Divisional Charts in Vedic Astrology (Varga Charts)

To calculate divisional charts (**Varga charts**), you need to divide each zodiac sign (30°) into a specific number of parts based on the divisional chart you're calculating. Each part is then mapped to a corresponding sign in the divisional chart.

Here's a **step-by-step guide** to calculate these charts manually and using astrology software like Jagannatha Hora or Parashara Light.

⚙️ General Formula for Divisional Chart Calculation

$$\text{Varga Position} = \left(\frac{\text{Planet's Degree in a Sign} \times \text{Number of Divisions}}{30}\right)$$

Key Variables:

- **Planet's Degree in Sign:** Exact position of the planet in the Rashi chart.

- **Number of Divisions:** Based on the Varga chart being calculated.

- **Final Position:** The degree and sign where the planet is placed in the corresponding divisional chart.

📚 Step-by-Step Calculation Process

🎯 Step 1: Identify the Planet's Position in Degrees

- Check the exact degree of the planet in the birth chart (D1).

- Example:

  - Venus is at **18°45'** in Taurus.

🎯 Step 2: Choose the Divisional Chart (Varga Chart)

Select the desired divisional chart and note the number of divisions.

Varga	Chart Name	Number of Divisions	Purpose
D2	Hora	2	Wealth and sustenance
D3	Drekkana	3	Siblings and courage
D4	Chaturthamsa	4	Property and fortune
D7	Saptamsa	7	Progeny and children
D9	Navamsa	9	Marriage and spirituality
D10	Dasamsa	10	Career and profession
D12	Dwadashamsa	12	Parents and ancestors
D16	Shodashamsa	16	Vehicles and luxuries
D20	Vimsamsa	20	Spiritual practices
D24	Chaturvimsamsa	24	Education and learning
D27	Bhamsa	27	Strength and valor
D30	Trimsamsa	30	Misfortunes and dangers
D40	Khavedamsa	40	Ancestral blessings/curses
D45	Akshavedamsa	45	Mental and spiritual growth
D60	Shashtiamsa	60	Past life and karma

🎯 Step 3: Calculate the Division Position

Use the formula:

$$\text{Division Position} = \left(\frac{\text{Planet's Degree in Sign} \times \text{Number of Divisions}}{30}\right)$$

Example: Calculating for D9 (Navamsa Chart)

- Venus at **18°45'** in Taurus.

- Number of divisions for D9 = 9.

  $$\text{Division Position} = \frac{(18 + \frac{45}{60}) \times 9}{30}$$
  $$\text{Division Position} = \frac{(18.75) \times 9}{30} = \frac{168.75}{30} = 5.625$$

- The 5th division corresponds to **Virgo** in the Navamsa chart.

🎯 Step 4: Map to the Divisional Chart

- Count the divisions from the starting sign to locate the position in the divisional chart.

- In D9:

  - 1st division: Taurus

  - 2nd division: Gemini

  - 3rd division: Cancer

  - 4th division: Leo

  - **5th division: Virgo** ✅

📊 Manual Calculation for Common Divisional Charts

🌞 D2 – Hora Chart Calculation

- Divide each sign into 2 parts (15° each).

- Odd signs:

  - 0° – 15° = Sun's Hora (Leo)

  - 15° – 30° = Moon's Hora (Cancer)

- Even signs:

  - 0° – 15° = Moon's Hora (Cancer)

  - 15° – 30° = Sun's Hora (Leo)

👥 D3 – Drekkana Chart Calculation

- Divide each sign into 3 parts (10° each).

- Count from the original sign to map the divisions:

  - 0° – 10° = 1st Drekkana (same sign)

  - 10° – 20° = 2nd Drekkana (5th sign from the original sign)

  - 20° – 30° = 3rd Drekkana (9th sign from the original sign)

👧👦 D9 – Navamsa Chart Calculation

- Divide each sign into 9 parts (3°20' each).

- Count the divisions from the same sign in **movable signs**, from 9th sign in **fixed signs**, and from 5th sign in **dual signs**:

  - Aries, Cancer, Libra, Capricorn: Start from the same sign.

  - Taurus, Leo, Scorpio, Aquarius: Start from the 9th sign.

  - Gemini, Virgo, Sagittarius, Pisces: Start from the 5th sign.

🏠 D10 – Dasamsa Chart Calculation

- Divide each sign into 10 parts (3° each).

- Movable signs: Start from the same sign.

- Fixed signs: Start from the 9th sign.

- Dual signs: Start from the 5th sign.

🌀 D60 – Shashtiamsa Chart Calculation

- Divide each sign into 60 parts (0°30' each).

- Each part is assigned a different sign, and this chart reveals **past life karma.**

🖥️ Using Software for Divisional Charts

If you want to skip manual calculations, astrology software can generate all divisional charts accurately.

Popular Tools:

1. **Jagannatha Hora (JHora):** Free software, excellent for divisional charts.

2. **Parashara's Light:** Commercial software with advanced predictive features.

3. **AstroSage/Online Tools:** Offers free online chart calculations.

✅ Steps to Generate Varga Charts:

1. Enter birth details (date, time, place).

2. Select 'Divisional Charts' or 'Varga Charts' option.

3. View charts like D9, D10, D60, etc., for detailed analysis.

📢 Pro Tips for Interpretation:

1. **Confirm Promises:** Check for repeating patterns across D1, D9, and other divisional charts.

2. **Analyze Lordship:** The lord of the Lagna and house significators in divisional charts.

3. **Vargottama:** A planet in the same sign in D1 and D9 gains strength.

4. **Check Yogas:** Analyze yogas in divisional charts for deeper insights.

Would you like me to explain **specific chart calculations** or guide you on **how to interpret** divisional charts? 😊

🔍 How to Analyze Divisional Charts?

1. **Planetary Strength:** Check the dignity (exaltation, debilitation, own sign) of planets in the Varga charts.

2. **Aspects and Yogas:** Analyze planetary aspects and yogas in each divisional chart.

3. **Lagna Lord and House Lords:** Assess the strength and position of the Lagna Lord in the respective Varga chart.

4. **Dasha and Transits:** Use Dasha systems (like Vimshottari) and transits to correlate the events seen in divisional charts.

💡 Tips for Reading Divisional Charts:

-   Start with the Rashi chart (D1) and confirm indications with relevant divisional charts.

-   Give more importance to planets that are strong in multiple divisional charts.

-   Combine insights from multiple divisional charts for a holistic view.

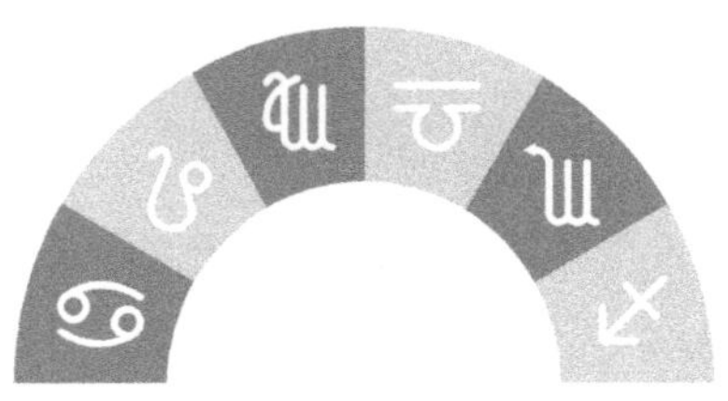

CHAPTER 5

The Dasha System (Planetary Periods) in Vedic Astrology

The **Dasha system** in Vedic astrology is a method used to **predict life events based on planetary periods**. It reveals the influence of different planets on a person's life at various stages, providing insights into **career, relationships, health, financial growth, and spiritual progress**.

Among various Dasha systems, the **Vimshottari Dasha** is the most widely used and considered the most accurate for understanding life patterns.

What is the Vimshottari Dasha System?

The **Vimshottari Dasha** is a **120-year planetary cycle** that divides human life into periods ruled by different planets. Each planet governs a specific number of years, influencing a person's life based on its **placement, strength, and aspects** in the birth chart (*Kundli*).

Planets and Their Dasha Periods in Vimshottari Dasha

Planet	Dasha Period (Years)	Key Themes During Dasha
Ketu	7	Detachment, spirituality, sudden changes
Venus	20	Love, luxury, relationships, artistic success
Sun	6	Authority, recognition, career growth

Planet	Dasha Period (Years)	Key Themes During Dasha
Moon	10	Emotions, mental peace, family, travel
Mars	7	Action, aggression, leadership, energy
Rahu	18	Unexpected events, ambition, material gains
Jupiter	16	Wisdom, education, expansion, prosperity
Saturn	19	Discipline, struggles, slow but steady success
Mercury	17	Intelligence, communication, business success

How Does Vimshottari Dasha Work?

- The Dasha system **begins at birth** based on the position of the Moon in a specific Nakshatra (constellation).

- The first planetary period (*Dasha*) is ruled by the planet governing Nakshatra.

- The sequence of planetary periods follows the **fixed cycle of Vimshottari Dasha** (Ketu → Venus → Sun → Moon → Mars → Rahu → Jupiter → Saturn → Mercury).

- Each **major Dasha period (Mahadasha)** is further divided into **Antardashas (sub-periods)** of all planets, making predictions more precise.

Example: If a person is born with the Moon in **Rohini Nakshatra (ruled by the Moon)**, their **first Dasha** will be **Moon Mahadasha (10 years)**, followed by **Mars Mahadasha (7 years)**, and so on.

How Planetary Periods Affect Life Events

Each planet's Mahadasha significantly impacts various aspects of life, depending on:

✔ Its **placement in the birth chart** (*Kundli*).

✔ Its **relationship with the Ascendant (Lagna)*.

✔ Whether it is a **benefic or malefic planet** for the natives.

✔ Its **association with other planets** (aspects, conjunctions, or exchanges).

Effects of Each Mahadasha

1. Ketu Mahadasha (7 years) – Spiritual Awakening & Detachment

- Brings **spiritual transformation, loss of material desires, and internal struggles**.

- Can cause **sudden changes, losses, or mystical experiences**.

- Best period for **meditation, self-discovery, and spiritual growth**.

2. Venus Mahadasha (20 years) – Love, Luxury, and Comfort

- Bring **wealth, beauty, love, relationships, and artistic success**.

- Favors **marriage, romance, and material comforts**.

- If afflicted, can lead to **overindulgence, relationship issues, or financial troubles**.

3. Sun Mahadasha (6 years) – Power & Authority

- Brings **leadership, career success, fame, and confidence**.

- Favorable for **government jobs, politics, or high positions**.

- If weak, can lead to **ego clashes, health issues, or struggles with authority figures**.

4. Moon Mahadasha (10 years) – Emotions & Mental Peace

- Bring **emotional growth, travel, family bonds, and nurturing**.

- Favorable for a **career in arts, creativity, and public life**.

- If afflicted, can lead to **mental stress, mood swings, or emotional instability**.

5. Mars Mahadasha (7 years) – Energy & Aggression

- Bring **action, courage, military or sports success, and leadership**.

- Supports **business, entrepreneurship, and adventure**.

- If afflicted, can cause **anger issues, accidents, or conflicts**.

6. Rahu Mahadasha (18 years) – Unpredictable Changes & Ambition

- Bring **unexpected gains, foreign travels, sudden success, or failures**.

- Encourages **innovation, technology, and materialistic success**.

- If negative, can lead to **addictions, illusions, or deceptive activities**.

7. Jupiter Mahadasha (16 years) – Wisdom & Growth

- Bring **prosperity, knowledge, spiritual development, and guidance**.

- Favorable for **education, higher learning, and religious activities**.

- If weak, can lead to **overconfidence, laziness, or financial losses**.

8. Saturn Mahadasha (19 years) – Discipline & Hard Work

- Brings **delayed success, perseverance, discipline, and stability**.

- Encourages **hard work, responsibility, and long-term achievements**.

- If afflicted, can lead to **hardships, struggles, or isolation**.

9. Mercury Mahadasha (17 years) – Intelligence & Communication

- Brings **success in education, business, writing, and media**.

- Enhances **logic, reasoning, and financial skills**.

- If weak, can cause **nervous issues, overthinking, or deceitful tendencies**.

How to Use Vimshottari Dasha for Predictions?

1. **Identify the current Mahadasha (major planetary period)** running in your chart.

2. **Check the placement of that planet** in your birth chart—strong or weak? Benefic or malefic?

3. **Analyse Antardasha (sub-periods) within Mahadasha** to see how different planetary energies interact.

4. **Observe planetary transits (Gochar)**—major events often align with Dasha changes + transits.

5. **Perform remedies** if a challenging Dasha is active (mantras, fasting, gemstones, donations).

✻ Conclusion

The **Vimshottari Dasha system** is a powerful tool in **Vedic astrology** that reveals how different planetary periods influence our life journey. While certain Dashas bring **success and prosperity**, others may cause **struggles and challenges**. However, with **self-awareness, effort, and astrological remedies**, one can navigate life more effectively and **make the best use of planetary influences**.

CHAPTER 6

Transit (Gochar) and Its Effects in Astrology

Astrology is a profound science that analyses celestial movements and their impact on human life. Among its many branches, transit (Gochar) astrology plays a crucial role in determining the effects of planets as they move through different zodiac signs and houses in an individual's birth chart.

What is Transit (Gochar)?

In Vedic astrology, "Gochar" refers to the current movement of planets in the sky about a person's natal chart (Janma Kundali). While a birth chart is a fixed representation of planetary positions at the time of birth, transits describe the continuous motion of these planets and their influences as they pass through different zodiac signs and houses.

Importance of Transit in Astrology

Transits indicate periods of growth, challenges, and transformation in a person's life. While Dasha (planetary periods) determines long-term life trends, transits act as short-term triggers that activate karmic events. Major life changes such as career shifts, marriage, financial gains, or struggles often coincide with significant planetary transits.

Effects of Different Planetary Transits

Each planet has a distinct influence depending on its nature, strength, and placement in a particular house and sign during transit.

1. Sun (Surya) Transit

- The Sun changes its sign every 30 days (approximately).

- It represents authority, health, and self-confidence.

- A favorable Sun transit brings recognition, leadership, and vitality.

- Unfavorable placement may cause ego clashes, health issues, or conflicts with authority figures.

2. Moon (Chandra) Transit

- The Moon moves fast and changes signs every 2.5 days.

- It governs emotions, mental peace, and family matters.

- A positive Moon transit enhances intuition, emotional stability, and happiness.

- A weak Moon transit can lead to mood swings, stress, and anxiety.

3. Mars (Mangal) Transit

- Mars transits a sign every 45 days.

- It influences energy, courage, and aggression.

- A strong Mars transit brings motivation, success in competition, and physical strength.

- A negative transit may lead to aggression, accidents, or conflicts.

4. Mercury (Budh) Transit

- Mercury moves quickly and stays in a sign for about 25 days.

- It controls intellect, communication, and business.

- A well-placed Mercury transit improves speech, logic, and financial gains.

- An afflicted Mercury can cause misunderstandings, nervousness, or financial instability.

5. Jupiter (Guru) Transit

- Jupiter changes signs every 12 to 13 months.

- It is the planet of wisdom, growth, and fortune.

- A good Jupiter transit brings expansion, prosperity, and spiritual progress.

- A weak Jupiter may cause delays, over-optimism, or financial setbacks.

6. Venus (Shukra) Transit

- Venus transits a sign approximately every 25-30 days.

- It governs love, relationships, and luxury.

- A favorable Venus transit enhances romance, beauty, and financial abundance.

- A negative transit can lead to relationship issues or indulgence in excess pleasures.

7. Saturn (Shani) Transit

- Saturn is a slow-moving planet, staying in one sign for 2.5 years.

- It is known as the "Karmic Planet" and teaches discipline, responsibility, and patience.

- A positive Saturn transit brings stability, hard-earned success, and wisdom.

- A difficult Saturn transit (like Sade Sati or Dhaiya) can bring struggles, delays, and hardships.

8. Rahu and Ketu Transit

- Rahu and Ketu are shadow planets, staying in a sign for 18 months.

- Rahu represents ambition, materialism, and desires, while Ketu signifies spirituality, detachment, and past-life karma.

- A favorable Rahu transit brings opportunities and breakthroughs, but an unfavorable one may cause confusion, illusions, and scandals.

- A strong Ketu transit enhances spirituality and intuition, while an afflicted Ketu can cause isolation and setbacks.

Major Transits and Their Impact

1. Saturn's Sade Sati and Dhaiya

- Sade Sati (7.5-year transit over the Moon sign) brings major life transformations, hardships, and learning experiences.

- Dhaiya (2.5-year Saturn transit over the 4th or 8th house from the Moon) can cause challenges in personal and professional life.

2. Jupiter's Transit Over Key Houses

- Jupiter's transit in the 1st, 5th, or 9th house brings good fortune, knowledge, and progress.

- In the 6th, 8th, or 12th house, it may cause financial losses or spiritual shifts.

3. Rahu-Ketu Return (18-Year Cycle)

- When Rahu and Ketu return to their natal positions, major karmic events unfold.

- This period often brings life-changing transformations, both positive and negative.

4. Eclipses and Their Effects

- Eclipses (Surya Grahan and Chandra Grahan) occur due to Rahu and Ketu and can cause sudden, intense life changes.

- People with their Sun, Moon, or Ascendant in eclipse-affected signs experience significant shifts.

How to Handle Challenging Transits?

While some transits bring blessings, others can be challenging. Here are some remedies to reduce their negative effects:

1. Worship and Mantras – Chanting mantras of afflicted planets can help balance their energies (e.g., Hanuman Chalisa for Saturn, Vishnu Stotra for Jupiter).

2. **Donations and Charity** – Donating items related to afflicted planets (e.g., black sesame for Saturn, yellow clothes for Jupiter) can bring relief.

3. **Fasting and Rituals** – Observing fasts on planetary days (e.g., Thursday for Jupiter, and Saturday for Saturn) helps mitigate bad transit effects.

4. **Gemstones and Yantras** – Wearing appropriate gemstones (with an astrologer's advice) can enhance favorable transits and neutralize difficult ones.

5. **Self-Discipline and Patience** – Hard transits teach valuable life lessons. Staying patient, working hard, and avoiding shortcuts can help navigate difficult times.

✦ Conclusion

Transit astrology (Gochar) is an essential tool for predicting life events and understanding planetary influences. While favorable transits bring growth and success, challenging ones provide opportunities for learning and self-improvement. By following remedies and aligning actions with planetary energies, one can make the most of cosmic influences and lead a balanced life.

How Transits Influence Daily Life

Astrology is not just about long-term predictions; it also plays a crucial role in shaping our daily experiences. Planetary transits (Gochar) influence our emotions, decisions, and external circumstances on a day-to-day basis. These celestial movements act as unseen forces, subtly directing our actions, moods, and interactions.

Understanding planetary transits can help us plan our days better, make informed decisions, and navigate life's challenges with greater awareness.

The Daily Impact of Planetary Transits

Every planet moves through the zodiac at a different speed, influencing different aspects of life daily. Some transits have short-term effects (like the Moon and Mercury), while others bring gradual shifts (like Jupiter and Saturn).

Let's explore how each planet's transit affects daily life:

1. The Moon: Emotions & Mood Swings

- The Moon changes signs every 2.5 days, making it the fastest-moving celestial body.

- It directly impacts emotions, mental state, and daily moods.

- A favorable Moon transit can bring happiness, clarity, and enthusiasm.

- An afflicted Moon transit may cause mood swings, anxiety, or emotional instability.

- Example: On a Full Moon day, people may feel more emotional, creative, or restless, while a New Moon can bring introspection and a desire for solitude.

2. The Sun: Energy & Confidence

- The Sun changes signs every month and affects self-expression, vitality, and leadership qualities.

- A strong Sun transit can boost confidence and motivation, making it a great time for new beginnings.

- A weak Sun transit might lead to lethargy, ego clashes, or a drop in self-esteem.

- Example: When the Sun transits Leo, people may feel more ambitious and assertive, whereas in Pisces, they may become more introspective and spiritual.

3. Mercury: Communication & Decision-Making

- Mercury moves every 25 days and governs thinking, communication, and travel.

- A well-placed Mercury transit enhances clarity, negotiation skills, and problem-solving abilities.

- Mercury retrograde (which happens three to four times a year) often causes misunderstandings, travel delays, and technical issues.

- Example: On a day when Mercury is well-placed, meetings and conversations flow smoothly, but during Mercury retrograde, people may face miscommunication or contract issues.

4. Venus: Relationships & Enjoyment

- Venus moves signs every 25–30 days and influences love, beauty, and pleasures.

- A strong Venus transit enhances romance, social interactions, and artistic creativity.

- A difficult Venus transit may lead to relationship misunderstandings, financial indulgence, or lack of harmony.

- Example: When Venus transits Libra, relationships flourish, and people feel more romantic and cooperative, whereas a Venus transit in Virgo might bring over-analysis and critical behavior in love matters.

5. Mars: Action & Motivation

- Mars stays in a sign for about 45 days, affecting energy levels, ambition, and physical activity.

- A favorable Mars transit increases productivity and determination, making it an excellent time to take action.

- A challenging Mars transit may cause frustration, aggression, or accidents.

- Example: When Mars transits Aries, people feel energetic and driven, but when Mars transits Cancer, energy may feel scattered, leading to emotional outbursts.

6. Jupiter: Growth & Opportunities

- Jupiter changes signs every 12–13 months and brings expansion, learning, and fortune.

- A positive Jupiter transit can open doors for success, financial gains, and spiritual growth.

- A negative Jupiter transit may cause overconfidence, laziness, or missed opportunities.

- Example: When Jupiter transits the 10th house in a personal chart, career growth is likely, whereas if it's in the 12th house, it may bring a focus on spiritual retreats or foreign travels.

7. Saturn: Challenges & Responsibilities

- Saturn moves every 2.5 years per sign and teaches discipline, patience, and perseverance.

- A well-placed Saturn transit brings stability, structure, and rewards for hard work.

- A difficult Saturn transit can create delays, obstacles, and a sense of burden.

- Example: When Saturn transits the 7th house, relationships may be tested for long-term commitment, while a Saturn transit in the 6th house may bring work-related stress but also career advancements.

8. Rahu & Ketu: Unexpected Events & Karmic Lessons

- These shadow planets stay in a sign for 18 months and bring sudden, karmic changes.

- Rahu represents obsession and material desires, while Ketu brings detachment and spiritual growth.

- Their transits can trigger unexpected life shifts, confusion, or breakthroughs.

- Example: A Rahu transit in the 10th house may bring sudden career growth, but with uncertainty and challenges, while a Ketu transit in the 4th house may lead to changes in home life or emotional detachment.

Real-Life Scenarios: How Transits Shape Daily Experiences

Here are some common ways transits influence everyday life:

1. Work and Productivity

- A strong Mars or Sun transit boosts energy and helps in tackling important projects.

- A Mercury retrograde may cause miscommunication at work, requiring extra caution in emails and contracts.

- A Saturn transit in the 6th house may increase workload but eventually lead to career growth.

2. Love and Relationships

- A Venus transit through the 5th or 7th house brings romance and new relationships.

- A difficult Mars or Saturn transit may lead to arguments or separation.

- A Moon transit in Cancer or Pisces makes people more sensitive and nurturing in relationships.

3. Financial Decisions

- A Jupiter transit in the 2nd or 11th house can bring financial gains.

- A Rahu transit in the 8th house may lead to unexpected expenses.

- A Venus transit in Taurus can make people spend more on luxury and pleasure.

4. Health and Well-Being

- A Moon transit in Scorpio can bring emotional stress and a need for relaxation.

- A Saturn transit in the 1st or 6th house can highlight health issues, requiring discipline in diet and exercise.

- A Mars transit in Aries or Leo provides extra stamina for physical activities.

How to Use Transit Astrology in Daily Life?

1. Check the Moon Sign Daily: Since the Moon governs emotions, knowing which sign it's in helps predict mood swings and energy levels.

2. Plan Important Events During Favorable Transits: Good Jupiter, Sun, and Venus transits are ideal for job interviews, financial investments, or social gatherings.

3. Avoid Risky Actions During Difficult Transits: During Mars or Mercury retrograde, it's best to avoid impulsive decisions, conflicts, or major purchases.

4. Use Remedies for Challenging Transits: Mantras, fasting, and charity can help mitigate the negative effects of transits like Saturn's Sade Sati or Rahu-Ketu periods.

Conclusion

Planetary transits continuously shape our daily lives, influencing our thoughts, emotions, and actions. By understanding their impact, we can align our efforts with cosmic energies, making informed choices for success and well-being. Instead of fearing difficult transits, we should see them as opportunities for growth, learning, and transformation.

Understanding Saturn's Sade Sati and Jupiter's Transit

Astrology plays a vital role in shaping our destiny, and among all planetary transits, Saturn's Sade Sati and Jupiter's transit are two of the most significant cycles that impact an individual's life. While Saturn's Sade Sati is known for bringing challenges, discipline, and transformation, Jupiter's transit is associated with growth, wisdom, and expansion. Understanding these two powerful planetary movements can help individuals navigate life's ups and downs with better awareness and preparedness.

Part 1: Saturn's Sade Sati – The Test of Time

What is Sade Sati?

Sade Sati is a 7.5-year transit of Saturn (Shani) over an individual's Moon sign (Janma Rashi) in their birth chart. The term "Sade Sati" means seven and a half years in Sanskrit (Sade – 2.5, Sati – 7.5). This period is considered a time of trials, personal transformation, and karmic cleansing.

Phases of Sade Sati

Sade Sati occurs in three phases, each lasting 2.5 years, as Saturn moves through three zodiac signs:

1. First Phase (Before the Moon Sign – Dhanur Bhukti)

- Begins when Saturn enters the 12th house from the natal Moon sign.

- Causes detachment, financial instability, or changes in residence.

- A time for introspection and preparation.

2. Second Phase (Over the Moon Sign – Janma Bhukti)

- Saturn transits directly over the natal Moon sign.

- The most intense phase, affecting emotions, mental peace, and relationships.

- Teaches patience, perseverance, and responsibility.

3. Third Phase (After the Moon Sign – Vyaya Bhukti)

- Saturn moves into the 2nd house from the natal Moon.

- Challenges related to wealth, family, and speech.

- Begins the process of stability and recovery.

Effects of Sade Sati

Sade Sati can bring difficulties, but it is also a period of self-growth and karmic cleansing. The intensity of its effects depends on:

- Saturn's position in the birth chart.

- The strength of the natal Moon.

- Other planetary influences.

Common Challenges During Sade Sati:

✓ Delays and obstacles in career and personal life.

✓ Emotional distress, loneliness, or depression.

✓ Financial instability and losses.

✓ Health issues or fatigue.

✓ Difficulties in relationships and family matters.

Positive Transformations from Sade Sati:

✓ Teaches discipline, patience, and hard work.

✓ Removes unnecessary attachments and illusions.

✓ Strengthens spirituality and wisdom.

✓ Helps build long-term stability and maturity.

Who is Most Affected by Sade Sati?

- People with Moon in Capricorn, Aquarius, or Pisces will experience Sade Sati in the coming years.

- Those with Saturn as a strong or ruling planet (e.g., Capricorn and Aquarius ascendants) may handle Sade Sati better.

- If Saturn is well-placed in the birth chart, the challenges of Sade Sati may turn into opportunities.

Remedies for Sade Sati

Since Saturn rewards hard work and discipline, the best way to navigate Sade Sati is to embrace patience and perseverance. However, some remedies can help:

- ✓ **Worship Lord Hanuman and Lord Shani:** Reciting Hanuman Chalisa and visiting Shani temples can reduce hardships.

- ✓ **Charity and Service:** Donating black sesame seeds, mustard oil, or feeding the poor helps pacify Saturn's effects.

- ✓ **Gemstones and Yantras:** Wearing a Blue Sapphire (Neelam) (if astrologically suitable) can strengthen Saturn's positive impact.

- ✓ **Self-Discipline and Hard Work:** Accept responsibilities and maintain integrity in work and relationships.

Part 2: Jupiter's Transit – The Path to Growth

What is Jupiter's Transit?

Jupiter (Guru) is the planet of wisdom, expansion, prosperity, and divine blessings. It transits each zodiac sign every 12–13 months, influencing personal growth, wealth, education, and spiritual evolution.

Jupiter's Transit Cycle

Since Jupiter completes one full revolution around the zodiac every 12 years, it returns to the same position in the birth chart approximately every 12 years, 24 years, 36 years, etc. This return often marks important life phases.

How Jupiter's Transit Affects Different Houses?

Jupiter's effects vary depending on which house it is transiting the natal Moon or Ascendant.

Favorable Jupiter Transits:

☑ 1ˢᵗ House: Personal growth, confidence, and new beginnings.

☑ 2ⁿᵈ House: Financial gains, wealth accumulation, and family happiness.

☑ 5ᵗʰ House: Love, creativity, education, and childbirth.

☑ 7ᵗʰ House: Marriage, partnerships, and business growth.

☑ 9ᵗʰ House: Luck, travel, higher studies, and spiritual progress.

☑ 11ᵗʰ House: Financial success, networking, and wish fulfillment.

Challenging Jupiter Transits:

⚠ 6ᵗʰ House: Health issues, debt, and competition.

⚠ 8ᵗʰ House: Sudden losses, obstacles, and transformations.

⚠ 12ᵗʰ House: Expenses, isolation, or foreign travel.

Jupiter's Retrograde Motion

Jupiter goes retrograde for about 4 months each year, during which its results may be delayed, requiring extra effort to manifest success.

Remedies to Strengthen Jupiter

If Jupiter is weak or its transit is unfavourable, the following remedies can be beneficial:

☑ Worship Lord Vishnu or Guru Brihaspati: Chant "Om Brihaspataye Namah" or recite Vishnu Sahasranama.

☑ Fasting on Thursdays: Observing a fast and donating yellow food items (like bananas, turmeric, or gram dal) enhances Jupiter's blessings.

☑ Wear Yellow Sapphire (Pukhraj): If advised by an astrologer, wearing Yellow Sapphire in gold on the index finger can strengthen Jupiter's positive influence.

☑ Engage in Charity and Teaching: Teaching, donating books, or helping students improves Jupiter's blessings.

Comparing Sade Sati and Jupiter's Transit

Aspect	Saturn's Sade Sati	Jupiter's Transit
Duration	7.5 years	12–13 months per sign
Nature	Tests, challenges, discipline	Growth, wisdom, fortune
Effects	Hardships, patience, transformation	Expansion, success, learning
Best Remedies	Hard work, Hanuman worship, patience	Charity, knowledge, devotion

❈ Conclusion

While Sade Sati teaches life lessons through discipline and endurance, Jupiter's transit brings opportunities for growth and success. Both these planetary transits play a crucial role in shaping an individual's life, and understanding them can help navigate challenges and maximize opportunities. Instead of fearing these transits, one should use them as stepping stones for personal and spiritual evolution.

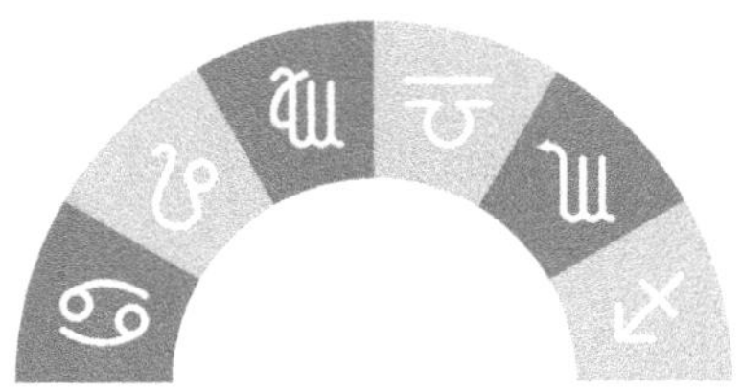

CHAPTER 7

Basic Predictions Using a Birth Chart

Introduction to the Birth Chart

Goal: Introduce what a birth chart is and why it's useful for prediction.

Key Points:

- A **birth chart** (natal chart) is a snapshot of the sky at the exact moment and location of your birth.

- It maps the positions of the **Sun, Moon, planets, and rising sign**, showing potential traits, strengths, challenges, and life themes.

- Used for both **personality insight** and **basic forecasting** (predictive astrology).

- Three pillars of interpretation:

    1. **Planets** = what's happening

    2. **Signs** = how it's expressed

    3. **Houses** = where in life it plays out

Example: Venus in Aries in the 5th house = Fast-moving love life, passionate about romance and creative expression.

Planets and Their Predictive Meaning

Goal: Understand the function of each planet in basic forecasting.

Key Points:

- **Personal Planets (Sun, Moon, Mercury, Venus, Mars)** – Show everyday experiences and personal traits.

- **Social Planets (Jupiter, Saturn)** – Indicate growth, discipline, and life lessons.

- **Outer Planets (Uranus, Neptune, Pluto)** – Indicate generational trends and deep transformation.

Short Planet Guide:

- **Sun** – Life purpose, vitality

- **Moon** – Emotions, instincts

- **Mercury** – Thinking, communication

- **Venus** – Love, beauty, relationships

- **Mars** – Action, drive, conflict

- **Jupiter** – Luck, growth

- **Saturn** – Structure, responsibility

- **Uranus** – Change, innovation

- **Neptune** – Dreams, illusions

- **Pluto** – Power, transformation

Example Prediction: Mars in Capricorn = Strong ambition, likely success in structured careers like business or engineering.

Signs and How Energy Is Expressed

Goal: Understand how signs modify planetary energy.

Key Points:

- Each planet sits in a **zodiac sign**, coloring how it behaves.

- The **element** (fire, earth, air, water) and **modality** (cardinal, fixed, mutable) influence style.

- Signs don't act alone—they shape the planet's expression.

Sign	Element	Style
Aries	Fire	Bold, direct
Taurus	Earth	Steady, sensual
Gemini	Air	Talkative, curious
Cancer	Water	Emotional, nurturing
Leo	Fire	Confident, dramatic
Virgo	Earth	Analytical, practical
Libra	Air	Diplomatic, fair
Scorpio	Water	Intense, secretive
Sagittarius	Fire	Adventurous, blunt
Capricorn	Earth	Ambitious, serious
Aquarius	Air	Inventive, aloof
Pisces	Water	Dreamy, intuitive

Example: Mercury in Pisces → communicates with imagination and empathy; might struggle with facts but excels in storytelling or spiritual insight.

Houses – Areas of Life Impacted

Goal: Learn how the **12 houses** reveal where in life each planet operates.

Key Points:

- Think of the chart as a wheel divided into 12 slices – each house rules a life area.

- Planets in houses show where your energy, challenges, and opportunities are.

Quick House Guide:

1. **Self, personality**

2. **Money, possessions**

3. **Communication, siblings**

4. **Home, family**

5. **Creativity, romance, kids**

6. **Health, daily work**

7. **Relationships, partnerships**

8. **Sex, shared money, transformation**

9. **Travel, higher learning**

10. **Career, reputation**

11. **Friendships, goals**

12. **Spirituality, secrets**

Example Prediction: Moon in the 6th house = Emotionally tied to work or health routines; prone to stress if routines are chaotic.

Aspects – Planetary Interactions

Goal: Teach how aspects show harmony or conflict between energies.

Key Points:

- Aspects are angles between planets, influencing how they interact.

- **Major Aspects:**

    ○ **Conjunction (0°)** – Powerfully blends energies

    ○ **Sextile (60°)** – Opportunities, harmony

    ○ **Square (90°)** – Tension, challenge

    ○ **Trine (120°)** – Easy flow, talent

    ○ **Opposition (180°)** – Polarity, balancing act

Interpreting Aspects:

- Consider the planets involved and the aspect's nature.

- Hard aspects = challenges or lessons.

- Soft aspects = natural gifts or ease.

Example Prediction: Venus square Saturn → Struggles in love or self-worth; learns maturity in relationships over time.

Making Basic Predictions + Transits

Goal: Teach the first step into forecasting using birth chart + current transits.

Key Points:

- Birth chart = blueprint; **transits** = current planetary movement affecting your chart.

- Predictions come from:

  ○ Current planets activating natal ones

  ○ Key planetary returns (e.g., Saturn return ~ age 29–30)

  ○ Personal triggers (e.g., New Moons in key houses)

Basic Prediction Steps:

1. Identify the natal placement (e.g., Jupiter in 2nd house)

2. Look at upcoming transits (e.g., Jupiter transiting 10th house)

3. Combine meanings: Growth (Jupiter) in career/public life (10th house) = job expansion, recognition.

Example: Transiting Saturn conjunct natal Venus in 7th house → tests in love or partnerships; may require commitment or separation.

Importance of Lagna and Moon Sign for Analysis

Astrology offers numerous tools for interpreting human experience, but two components stand out for their foundational role in birth chart analysis: the **Lagna** (Ascendant) and the **Moon sign**. While the Sun sign is popular in mainstream astrology, it is the Lagna and Moon sign that provide the nuanced layers needed for meaningful and accurate predictions. These two chart anchors allow astrologers to understand not just *what* happens in life, but *how* the individual is likely to experience and respond to it.

The Lagna : Foundation of the Natal Chart

The Lagna, also known as the Ascendant, is the zodiac sign that was rising on the eastern horizon at the exact moment of birth. This sign changes roughly every two hours, making it highly sensitive to birth time accuracy. The Lagna sets the orientation of the entire birth chart—it determines the placement of the twelve houses, which in turn govern the different areas of life such as career, relationships, home, and health.

The qualities of the Lagna sign and the condition of its ruling planet describe the person's physical vitality, personality style, behavior, and how they approach life's challenges. For instance, an individual with **Aries Lagna** will typically have a bold and assertive temperament, characterized by courage, directness, and a desire to lead. In contrast, someone with **Libra Lagna** may approach the world through charm, negotiation, and a strong sense of fairness, with Venus as the ruler emphasizing beauty and social harmony.

The strength of the Ascendant and its ruling planet (called the **Lagna lord**) is critical in predicting the overall robustness of life. A well-placed Lagna lord, receiving supportive aspects from benefic planets, often grants resilience, clarity of purpose, and positive life momentum. Conversely, if the Lagna or its lord is weak, afflicted, or placed in difficult houses, the native may experience confusion, vulnerability, or a lack of direction.

Astrologically, the Lagna acts as the "body" or vessel of life. It shows how the external world perceives the individual and how they present themselves. More importantly, it is the basis for **house-based predictions**, which are central to forecasting specific life events. For example, if Saturn transits the tenth house from the Lagna, career responsibilities or restructuring may occur. If the Lagna is miscalculated, such interpretations lose accuracy.

The Moon Sign : Mirror of the Inner World

While the Lagna represents the physical and behavioral layer of the self, the **Moon sign** delves into the emotional and psychological realm.

The Moon is a symbol of the mind, memory, feelings, and the subtle undercurrents of consciousness. In Vedic astrology, it holds even greater predictive weight than the Sun, because the Moon governs one's *manas*—the seat of emotions, instincts, and subjective experience.

Unlike the Sun, which stays in each sign for about a month, the Moon changes signs every 2.5 days. This fast movement makes the Moon highly personal, reflecting not just what a person does, but how they feel about what they do. It also governs habits, needs for emotional security, and unconscious patterns. The Moon sign influences daily mood, receptivity, and how one processes and expresses emotion.

For example, a person with **Moon in Cancer** tends to be deeply nurturing, emotionally responsive, and protective of loved ones. Their decisions are often guided by intuition and the desire for comfort and familiarity. By contrast, **Moon in Aquarius** may indicate a person who feels safest when maintaining emotional distance and engaging with ideas rather than sentiments.

From a predictive standpoint, the Moon sign plays a crucial role in **timing events**. Systems like the **Vimshottari Dasha**—a powerful life-period system in Vedic astrology—are entirely based on the Moon's position at birth. The Moon sign also determines one's **Nakshatra** (lunar mansion), which adds another layer of depth in analyzing personal behavior, compatibility, and karmic influences.

One of the most well-known predictive cycles, **Sade Sati**, is a 7.5-year period of Saturn's transit over the Moon sign and its adjacent signs. It is known to bring emotional challenges, psychological restructuring, and significant life shifts. Its intensity is felt directly through the Moon—the mind—and not through outer events alone.

Lagna and Moon : Two Pillars of Predictive Astrology :

In practical astrology, both the Lagna and Moon sign must be integrated to form a complete picture. Each plays a vital yet distinct role in both personality analysis and prediction.

The **Lagna** represents the external self—how life is navigated, where major life themes will occur, and how others see the native. It is often the preferred starting point for evaluating **career paths**, **health**, **status**, and **long-term life direction**.

The **Moon sign**, on the other hand, rules the inner self—how experiences are emotionally processed, what triggers joy or sorrow, and how the person copes with change. It becomes essential when analyzing **emotional well-being**, **family dynamics**, **mental patterns**, and **compatibility**.

In the context of **transits**, both are used for different kinds of forecasting. From the **Lagna**, one can predict where events are likely to occur—for example, a planet transiting the fourth house may bring changes in home or family. From the **Moon**, the same transit can reveal how emotionally turbulent or satisfying that change will feel. Both perspectives together create a fuller, richer understanding.

Astrologers often find that when the Lagna and Moon sign are in harmony—for example, both in compatible elements or aspects—the person is generally more aligned in their inner and outer world. When there is tension—such as a fiery Lagna and a watery, emotional Moon sign—the person may feel torn between action and sensitivity, confidence and vulnerability.

Ultimately, the Lagna and Moon sign are not in competition; they are complementary tools. When used together, they allow the astrologer to address both the **situation** and the **response**, the **event** and the **experience**. For serious students of astrology, understanding these two pillars is not optional—it is essential.

Checking Career, Marriage and Health from a Horoscope

A horoscope, or natal chart, offers a comprehensive view of an individual's life through the positions of the planets at the time of birth. Among the many areas astrology explores, **career**, **marriage**, and **health** are often the most sought-after. While advanced predictions require a nuanced understanding of multiple chart factors, even a basic approach can yield clear insights into a person's life direction, relationship patterns, and physical well-being. This section offers a structured guide to analyzing these three key areas in a birth chart.

Under standing the Frame work – The Houses and Planets Involved

Before examining career, marriage, or health in detail, one must understand the **houses**, **planets**, and **signs** associated with these life areas:

Key Houses:

- **Career:** 10th house (profession, status), 6th house (daily work), and 2nd house (income)

- **Marriage:** 7th house (partnership), 2nd house (family life), 11th house (fulfillment)

- **Health:** 1st house (body), 6th house (illnesses), 8th house (chronic or sudden issues), 12th house (hospitalization)

Key Planets:

- **Sun** – Vitality, authority (career, health)

- **Moon** – Emotional well-being (marriage, health)

- **Mercury** – Communication and intellect (career)

- **Venus** – Love, marriage, luxury

- **Mars** – Energy, drive, aggression (career, health)

- **Jupiter** – Wisdom, expansion (career, marriage)

- **Saturn** – Discipline, limitations, long-term issues (career delays, health problems)

Lagna (Ascendant):

Always consider the **Ascendant** and its lord, as this sets the stage for interpreting the rest of the chart. A strong Lagna and Lagna lord usually indicate resilience and positive life outcomes.

Career – Profession, Success and Direction

Career analysis starts primarily from the **10th house**, also called the *Karma Bhava*, which represents one's actions, ambitions, and public reputation.

Step-by-Step Career Analysis:

1. **Assess the 10th House:**

   - Check the sign on the 10th house.

   - Analyze the condition of its **ruling planet**.

   - Note any **planets placed** in the 10th house—benefics like Jupiter or Mercury enhance it; malefics like Saturn or Mars may bring delays or struggles but also discipline.

2. **Examine the 6th and 2nd Houses:**

   - The 6th shows how a person handles work, challenges, and service.

   - The 2nd shows how the person earns, their speech, and wealth accumulation.

3. **Evaluate the 10th Lord:**

   - Where the 10th lord is placed indicates **career focus**.

   - For example, the 10th lord in the 5th house may suggest a career in education, creativity, or entertainment.

4. **Check for Yogas and Dasha Support:**

   - Look for **Raj Yogas**, **Dhana Yogas**, or **Karma Yogas** involving the 2nd, 6th, and 10th lords.

   - Examine the current **dasha (planetary period)** to see if career growth is supported.

Example: A person with **Sun in the 10th house** in Leo is likely to rise in authoritative positions—government, leadership, or public roles—due to natural charisma and ambition.

Marriage – Relationships, Love, and Compatability

Marriage is primarily examined through the **7th house**, which governs legal partnerships, romantic unions, and emotional compatibility. The **condition of the 7th house** and its ruler offers deep insight into one's marital life

Steps for marriage Analysis:

1. **Assess the 7th House and Its Lord:**

   ○ Identify the sign and analyze the **lord's strength, dignity, and placement.**

   ○ Planets **placed in the 7th house** affect marital dynamics:

     ▪ Venus/Jupiter → loving, supportive marriage

     ▪ Saturn → late marriage or karmic lessons

     ▪ Mars → passion but possible conflict (*Kuja Dosha*)

2. **Evaluate Venus and Jupiter:**

   ○ **Venus** is the karaka (significator) for marriage, especially for men.

   ○ **Jupiter** is the marriage karaka for women.

   ○ Check their **strength**, **aspects**, and **dasha** periods for timing.

3. **Consider the Navamsa Chart (D9):**

   ○ In Vedic astrology, the **Navamsa chart** is crucial for marriage.

   ○ A strong D9 indicates stability and deeper compatibility.

4. **Timing Marriage:**

   ○ Favorable **dasha of 7th lord**, **Venus**, or **Jupiter** often brings marriage.

   ○ Transits over the 7th house or aspecting Venus can trigger unions.

Example: A native with **Jupiter in the 7th house** in Sagittarius may marry a wise, ethical partner and enjoy a traditional, respectful relationship.

Health – Vitality, Illness and Recovery

Health analysis is done primarily through the **1st house**, **6th house**, **8th house**, and **12th house**. A robust Lagna and Lagna lord generally signal strong constitution and immunity.

Health Analysis Steps:

1. **Examine the 1ˢᵗ House:**

   ○ Represents the body, overall vitality, and physical makeup.

   ○ Malefic influence (Saturn, Rahu, Mars) may reduce energy or cause chronic issues.

2. **Check the 6ᵗʰ House:**

   ○ Indicates diseases, particularly acute or lifestyle-related.

   ○ A strong 6ᵗʰ lord and benefic aspects can help resist or recover from illness.

3. **Analyze the 8ᵗʰ and 12ᵗʰ Houses:**

   ○ The 8ᵗʰ governs chronic illnesses, surgeries, and sudden health issues.

   ○ The 12ᵗʰ relates to hospitals, isolation, and sleep patterns.

4. **Planetary Karakas for Health:**

   ○ **Sun** = general vitality, heart

   ○ **Moon** = mental health, fluids

   ○ **Saturn** = bones, chronic illness

   ○ **Mars** = blood, injury

   ○ **Mercury** = nerves, skin

5. **Timing of Illness:**

   ○ Examine adverse **dashas** of malefic planets, especially if they are connected to the 6ᵗʰ, 8ᵗʰ, or 12ᵗʰ houses.

   ○ Difficult **transits** (e.g., Saturn or Rahu over Lagna or Moon) may lower immunity.

Example: A person with **Saturn in the 6ᵗʰ house** in Virgo may face chronic digestive or bone-related issues but can manage well with discipline and routine.

Integrating Career, Marriage and Health _ A Holistic Approach

Although each area—career, marriage, and health—has its designated houses and planets, they are deeply interconnected. Career stress can affect health. Health issues may delay marriage. Relationship struggles may influence career motivation. Thus, a **holistic reading** should connect these life areas rather than isolate them.

General Guidelines:

- Always begin with a **strong Lagna** and assess the overall planetary strength and dignity.

- Use the **Moon sign** to evaluate mental and emotional resilience across all areas.

- Look at the **current dasha and transits** to identify which area of life is currently activated.

- If multiple key houses (6th, 7th, 10th) are connected through aspects or conjunctions, that life theme may dominate the chart.

Example Holistic Case:

A chart with:

- Saturn in the 10th (slow career growth),

- Mars in the 7th (conflicts in marriage),

- Moon afflicted in the 6th (mental health issues)…would suggest a person whose ambition may lead to relationship friction and stress-related health concerns. However, if Jupiter is strong in the 9th or 1st house, the individual may find meaning and resilience through spiritual growth, counseling, or teaching.

Astrology's strength lies not just in forecasting events but in helping individuals **prepare, adapt, and grow** through their life patterns. When career, marriage, and health are seen as dynamic forces in a person's journey, the birth chart becomes a tool for deep insight and conscious evolution.

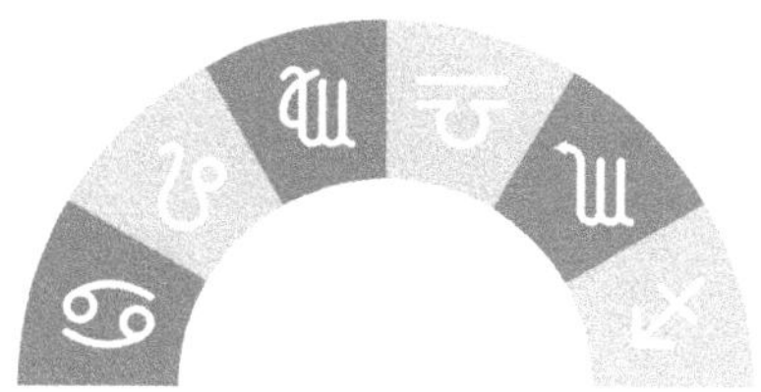

CHAPTER 8

Remedies in Vedic Astrology

Vedic Astrology is not just about predicting future events but also about providing effective remedies to balance planetary influences. Since 

planetary positions in a person's birth chart (Kundali) are linked to past karma, some combinations bring challenges, while others bring prosperity. Astrological remedies help mitigate negative effects and enhance positive energies, allowing individuals to lead a more harmonious life.

The remedies in Vedic astrology are based on mantras, rituals, donations, gemstones, yantras, fasting, and lifestyle adjustments. These practices help neutralize doshas (imbalances) and attract beneficial cosmic energies.

Types of Remedies in Vedic Astrology

1. Mantra Remedies – The Power of Sacred Sounds

Mantras are sacred syllables or phrases that generate vibrational energy to connect with planetary deities. Chanting specific mantras enhances the positive effects of benefic planets and reduces the negative impact of malefic planets.

Examples of Planetary Mantras:

Planet	Mantra	Benefits
☀ Sun (Surya)	*Om Hreem Suryaya Namah*	Improves confidence, success, and health.
☽ Moon (Chandra)	*Om Som Somaya Namah*	Balances emotions, and improves peace of mind.
♂ Mars (Mangal)	*Om Ang Angarakaya Namah*	Increases courage, and energy, and reduces aggression.
☿ Mercury (Budh)	*Om Bum Budhaya Namah*	Enhances intelligence, communication, and business.
♃ Jupiter (Guru)	*Om Brim Brihaspataye Namah*	Boosts wisdom, fortune, and spiritual growth.
♀ Venus (Shukra)	*Om Shum Shukraya Namah*	Enhances love, beauty, and creativity.
♄ Saturn (Shani)	*Om Sham Shanicharaya Namah*	Reduces hardships, and improves discipline and career.
☊ Rahu	*Om Rahave Namah*	Controls illusions, fear, and unexpected problems.
☋ Ketu	*Om Ketave Namah*	Enhances spiritual progress, and reduces negativity.

How to Chant Mantras Effectively?

✓ Chant 108 times daily using a Rudraksha mala.

✓ Preferably chant during the planet's hora (auspicious time).

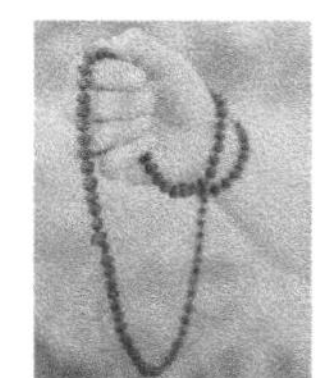

✓ Chant with devotion and correct pronunciation.

2. Gemstone Remedies – Enhancing Planetary Strength

Gemstones absorb cosmic energy and radiate it into the wearer's aura, strengthening weak planets in the birth chart. Wearing the right gemstone can help attract good luck and success.

Important Guidelines:

✓ Gemstones should be natural, unheated, and untreated for maximum effects.

✓ They must be prescribed by an experienced astrologer based on the birth chart.

✓ They should be worn on specific days and fingers, set in the right metal.

Planet	Gemstone	Metal	Finger	Best Day to Wear
☀ Sun	Ruby (Manikya)	Gold	Ring Finger	Sunday
☽ Moon	Pearl (Moti)	Silver	Little Finger	Monday
♂ Mars	Red Coral (Moonga)	Gold/Copper	Ring Finger	Tuesday
☿ Mercury	Emerald (Panna)	Gold/Silver	Little Finger	Wednesday
♃ Jupiter	Yellow Sapphire (Pukhraj)	Gold	Index Finger	Thursday
♀ Venus	Diamond (Heera) / White Sapphire	Platinum/ Silver	Middle Finger	Friday
♄ Saturn	Blue Sapphire (Neelam)	Silver/Iron	Middle Finger	Saturday
☊ Rahu	Hessonite (Gomed)	Silver	Middle Finger	Saturday
☋ Ketu	Cat's Eye (Lehsunia)	Silver	Middle Finger	Saturday

◈ **Caution:** Wearing the wrong gemstone can enhance negative planetary effects. Always consult an astrologer before wearing one.

3. Donation and Charity (Daan) – Neutralizing Karmic Effects

Daan (charity) is one of the most powerful remedies in Vedic astrology. It helps balance planetary influences by offering specific items related to afflicted planets.

Planet	Items for Donation	Best Day for Donation
☀ Sun	Wheat, Jaggery, Red Cloth	Sunday
☽ Moon	Rice, Milk, White Clothes	Monday
♂ Mars	Red Lentils, Copper, Mustard Oil	Tuesday
☿ Mercury	Green Gram, Books, Stationery	Wednesday

Planet	Items for Donation	Best Day for Donation
♃ Jupiter	Yellow Clothes, Turmeric, Sweets	Thursday
♀ Venus	White Flowers, Curd, Perfume	Friday
♄ Saturn	Black Sesame, Iron, Black Cloth	Saturday
☊ Rahu	Mustard, Coconut, Blue Clothes	Saturday
☋ Ketu	Brown Clothes, Horse Gram	Saturday

◈ **Best Practice: Donate with a pure heart, without expecting anything in return.**

4. Fasting (Vrat) – Balancing Planetary Energy

Fasting is a powerful remedy to strengthen planets and reduce their malefic effects.

Planet	Fasting Day	Recommended Food
☀ Sun	Sunday	Wheat, Jaggery, Fruits
☽ Moon	Monday	Milk, Rice, White Foods
♂ Mars	Tuesday	Lentils, Fruits
☿ Mercury	Wednesday	Green Leafy Vegetables, Fruits
♃ Jupiter	Thursday	Chana Dal, Banana, Yellow Foods
♀ Venus	Friday	Dairy, Sweets
♄ Saturn	Saturday	Black Sesame, Urad Dal
☊ Rahu	Saturday	Coconut, Mustard
☋ Ketu	Saturday	Horse Gram, Brown Foods

◈ **Tip: Drink plenty of water and maintain a pure mindset while fasting.**

5. Yantras and Rudraksha – Protective Shields

- **Yantras:** Sacred geometric diagrams that harness planetary energy.
- **Rudraksha:** Sacred beads that align energy with cosmic forces.

Examples:

✓ **Shani Yantra** – Reduces the negative effects of Saturn's Sade Sati.

✓ **Mahalakshmi Yantra** – Attracts wealth and prosperity.

✓ **1 Mukhi Rudraksha** – Enhances concentration and spiritual growth.

✓ **5 Mukhi Rudraksha** – Strengthens Jupiter's positive effects.

6. Pujas and Homas – Seeking Divine Blessings

Performing specific pujas (rituals) and homas (fire ceremonies) invokes planetary deities to bless and protect an individual.

✓ **Navagraha Puja** – Balances all planetary energies.

✓ **Maha Mrityunjaya Jaap** – Reduces suffering and improves health.

✓ **Rahu-Ketu Shanti Puja** – Neutralizes the effects of Rahu-Ketu doshas.

✨ Conclusion

Vedic astrology remedies are powerful tools to overcome challenges, enhance success, and maintain inner balance. By incorporating the right combination of mantras, fasting, gemstones, donations, and spiritual practices, one can align with cosmic energies and live a more fulfilling life. Instead of fearing planetary influences, we should use these remedies to harmonize our lives with the universe.

Importance of Charity and Rituals in Vedic Astrology

Charity (Daan) – The Act of Selfless Giving

Charity, or Daan, holds great significance in Vedic astrology and spiritual traditions. It is believed that donating with a pure heart helps neutralize past karma (Prarabdha Karma) and reduces the negative effects of malefic planets.

Why is Charity Important?

✓ **Balances Negative Planetary Effects** – Donating items associated with afflicted planets helps pacify their malefic influence.

✓ Attracts Positive Energy – Giving selflessly brings divine blessings and prosperity.

✓ Improves Karma – Acts of kindness contribute to good karma, shaping a brighter future.

✓ Removes Obstacles – Regular charity helps reduce financial struggles, health issues, and delays in life.

Planetary Charity Recommendations

Each planet is associated with specific items for donation:

Planet	Donation Items	Best Day
☀ Sun	Wheat, Jaggery, Red Cloth	Sunday
☽ Moon	Rice, Milk, White Clothes	Monday
♂ Mars	Red Lentils, Copper, Mustard Oil	Tuesday
☿ Mercury	Green Gram, Books, Stationery	Wednesday
♃ Jupiter	Yellow Clothes, Turmeric, Sweets	Thursday
♀ Venus	White Flowers, Curd, Perfume	Friday
♄ Saturn	Black Sesame, Iron, Black Cloth	Saturday
☊ Rahu	Coconut, Mustard Seeds, Blue Clothes	Saturday
☋ Ketu	Horse Gram, Brown Clothes	Saturday

Key Principle: Charity should be done selflessly, without expecting anything in return.

Rituals (Pujas & Homas) – Connecting with Divine Energies

Rituals in Vedic astrology include Pujas (worship), Homas (fire ceremonies), and Mantra chanting, which help in strengthening planetary energies and seeking divine guidance.

Why are Rituals Important?

✓ Removes Doshas (Afflictions) – Rituals like Navagraha Puja help balance planetary energies.

✓ Enhances Spiritual Growth – Regular prayers and homas connect individuals with cosmic forces.

✓ Attracts Prosperity & Protection – Specific rituals invoke divine blessings for success, health, and peace.

Popular Rituals & Their Benefits

✓ Maha Mrityunjaya Homa – Protection from diseases and untimely death.

✓ Rahu-Ketu Shanti Puja – Reduces the effects of Kaal Sarp Dosh and Rahu-Ketu afflictions.

✓ Shani Puja – Helps during Sade Sati and reduces hardships.

✓ Lakshmi Puja – Attracts wealth and financial stability.

✤ Conclusion

Charity and rituals are powerful tools in Vedic astrology that help individuals mitigate negative karma, attract prosperity, and achieve spiritual growth. By practicing selfless giving and following proper rituals, one can align with cosmic energies and lead a harmonious, fulfilling life.

Conclusion: Your Journey Through the Stars ✴

Congratulations on completing your journey through the fascinating world of astrology! You've explored the zodiac signs, planetary influences, houses, and aspects, learning how they shape personalities, relationships, and life experiences. By now, you have the tools to interpret birth charts, understand astrological patterns, and even apply this knowledge in your daily life.

Astrology is not just about predicting the future—it's about gaining insight, fostering self-awareness, and deepening your connection with the universe. Whether you're using it to understand yourself better, strengthen your relationships, or simply appreciate the cosmic rhythms that influence our lives, astrology offers endless possibilities for growth and discovery.

As you continue exploring, remember that astrology is a lifelong journey. The more you practice and observe, the deeper your understanding will become. Trust your intuition, stay curious, and allow the stars to guide you toward greater self-discovery.

Thank you for allowing this book to be part of your journey. May your path be illuminated by the wisdom of the cosmos. ✴

References

1. Parashara, M. (n.d.). Brihat Parashara Hora Shastra (R. Santhanam, Trans.). Sagar Publications.

2. Varahamihira. (1993). Brihat Samhita (P. S. Sastri, Trans.). Ranjan Publications.

3. Raman, B. V. (1992). How to Judge a Horoscope (Vols. 1 & 2). UBS Publishers.

4. Rao, K. N. (1999). Learn Hindu Astrology Easily. Vani Publications.

Disclaimer

The information provided in *"Easy Astrology: Learn in Simple Steps"* is intended for educational and entertainment purposes only. While astrology can offer valuable insights into personality traits, relationships, and life patterns, it should not be considered a substitute for professional advice, including but not limited to medical, psychological, legal, or financial guidance.

The interpretations and techniques shared in this book are based on traditional astrological principles and the author's knowledge. However, results and experiences may vary for each individual. Readers are encouraged to use their own judgment and discretion when applying the concepts presented.

The author and publisher disclaim any liability for decisions made based on the information provided in this book. By reading and applying the content, you agree that any actions you take are solely your responsibility.

Astrology is a tool for self-discovery and reflection—enjoy the journey, but always trust your own intuition and knowledge as you explore the stars! ✸